AF606651

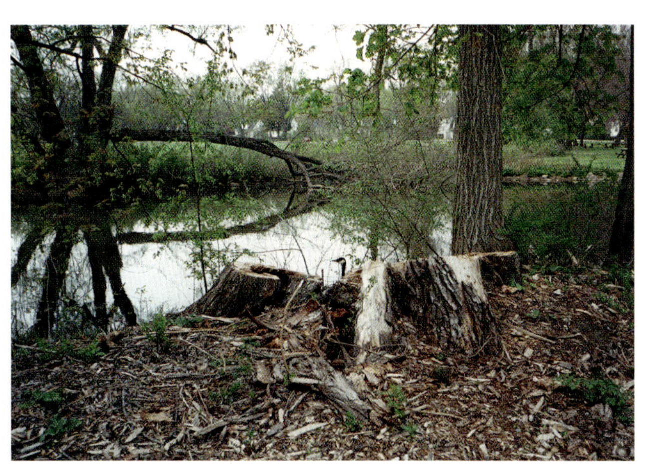

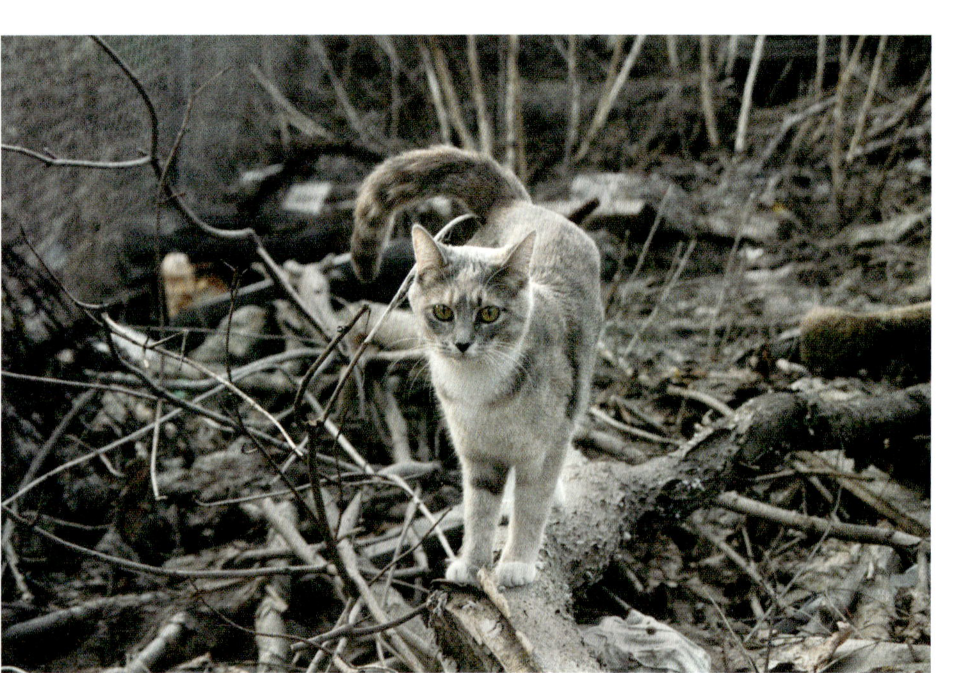

ANIMALS THAT SAW ME

ESSAY BY

Timothy Morton

Ed Panar

Volume Two

THE ICE PLANT Los Angeles 2016

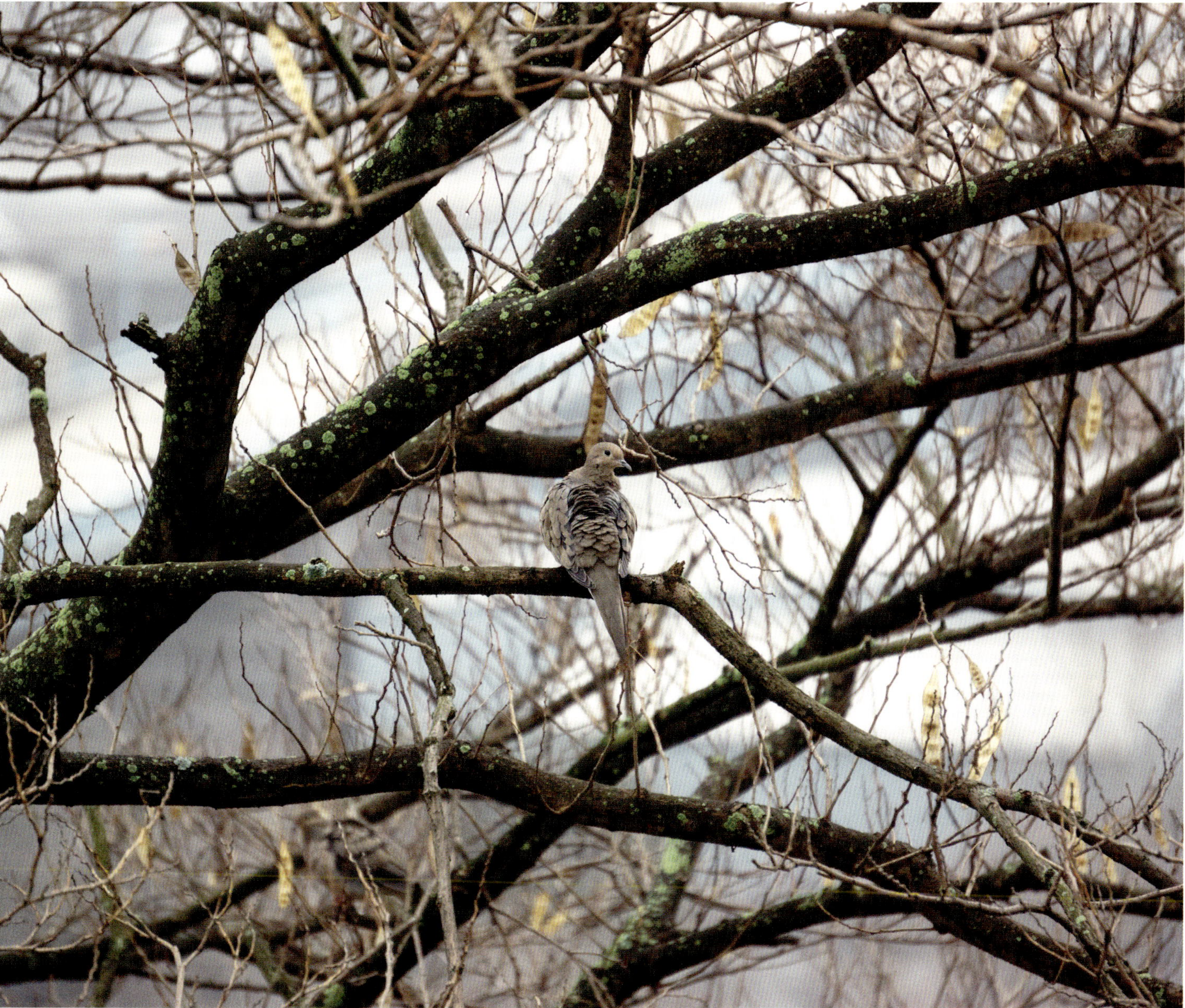

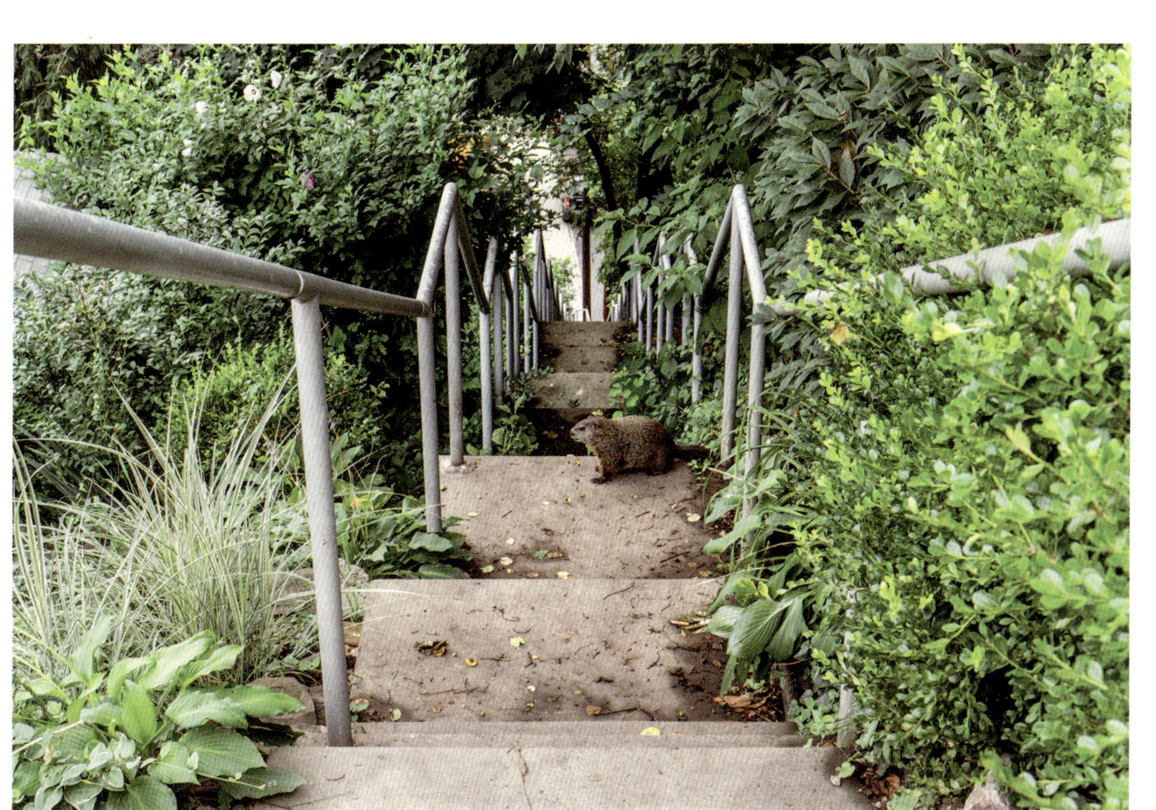

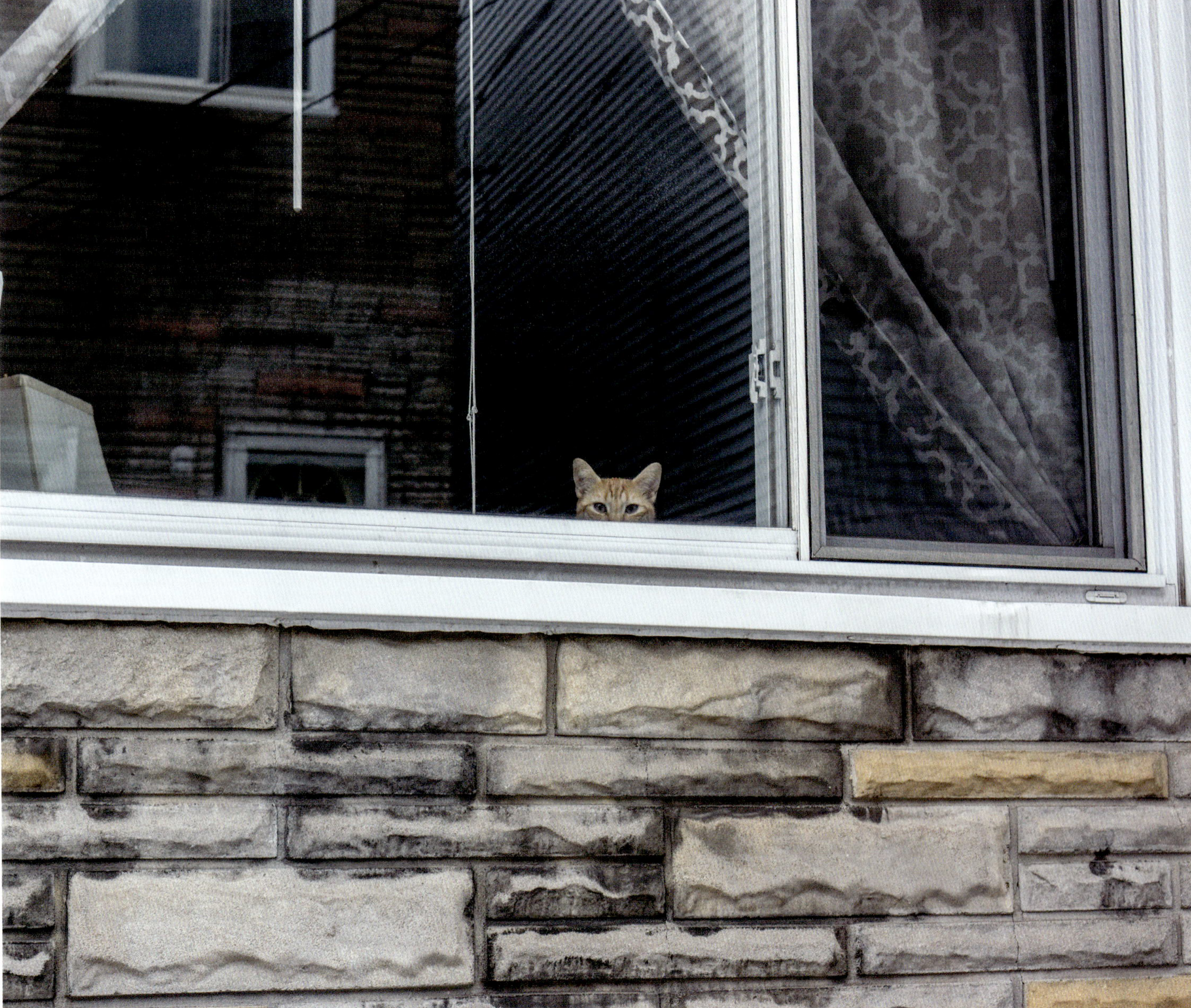

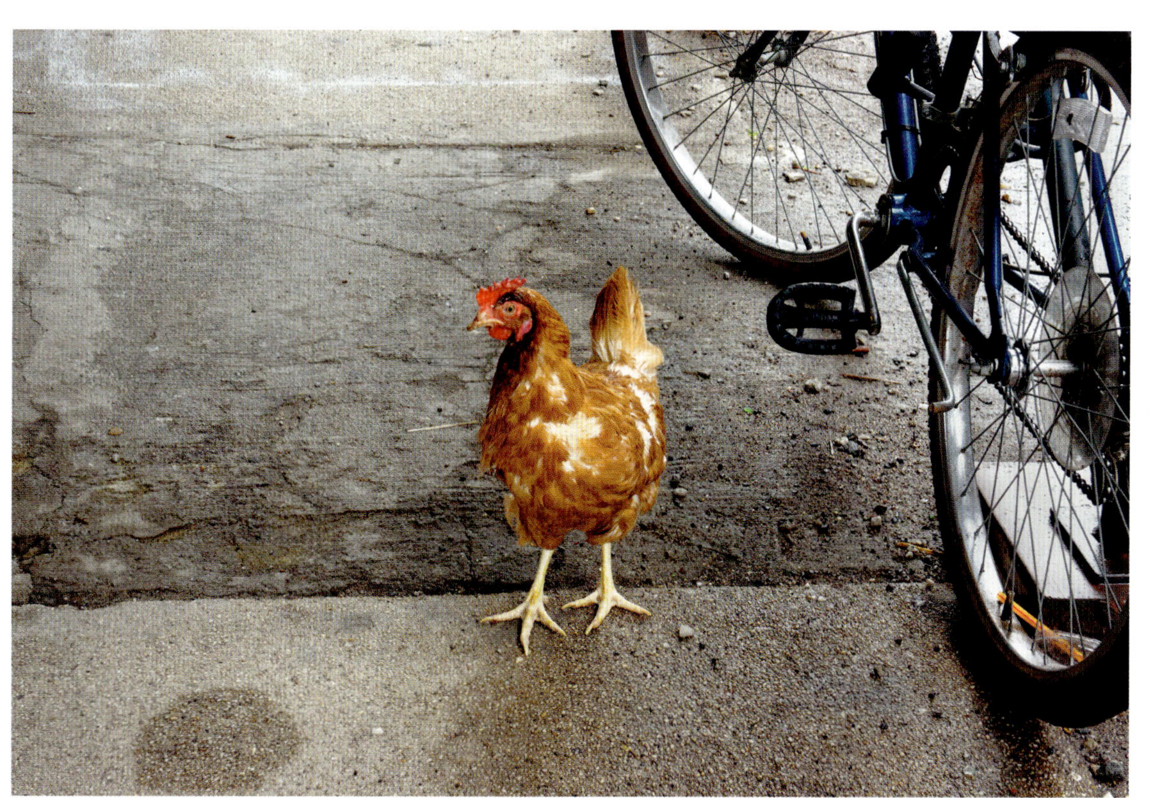

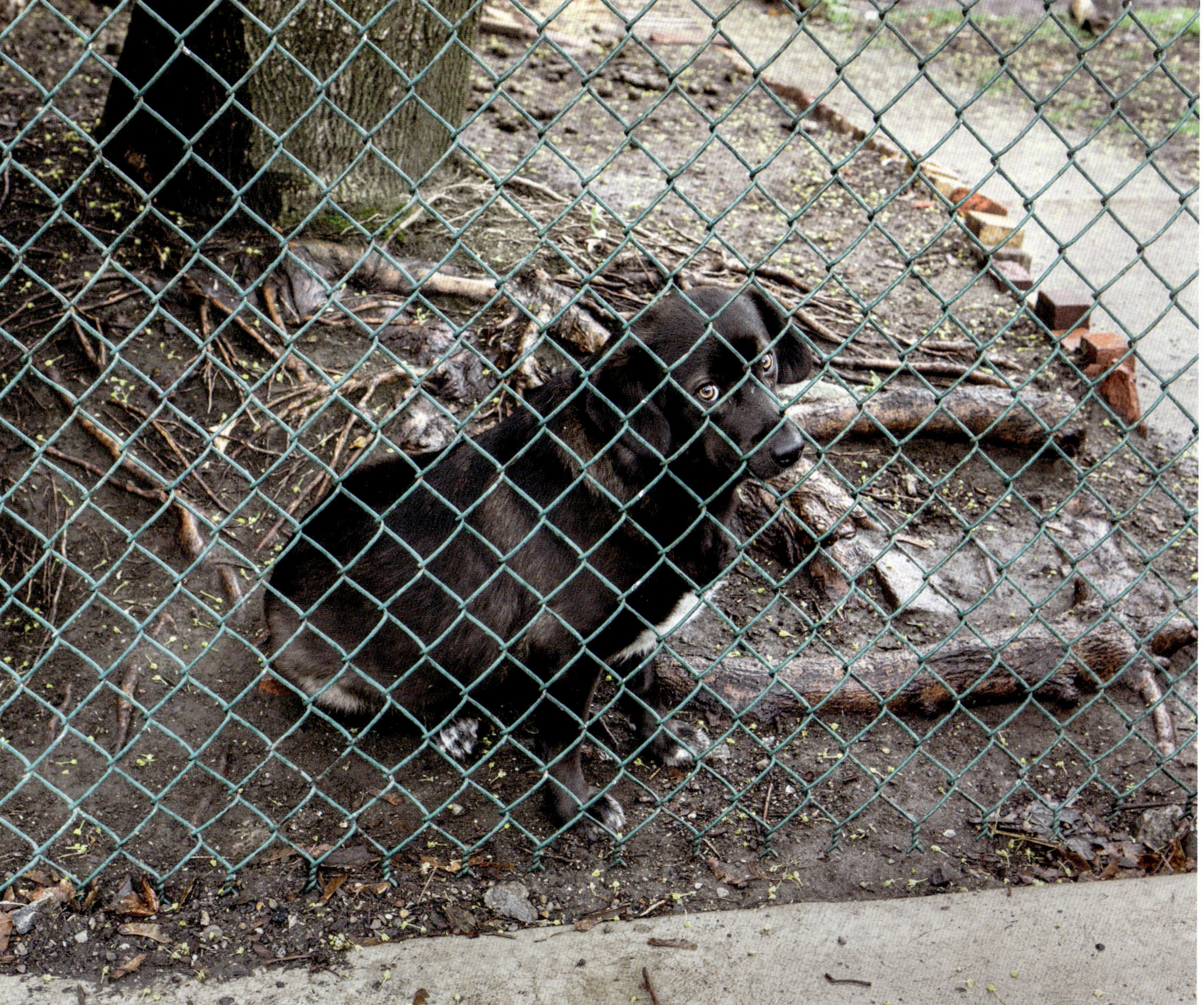

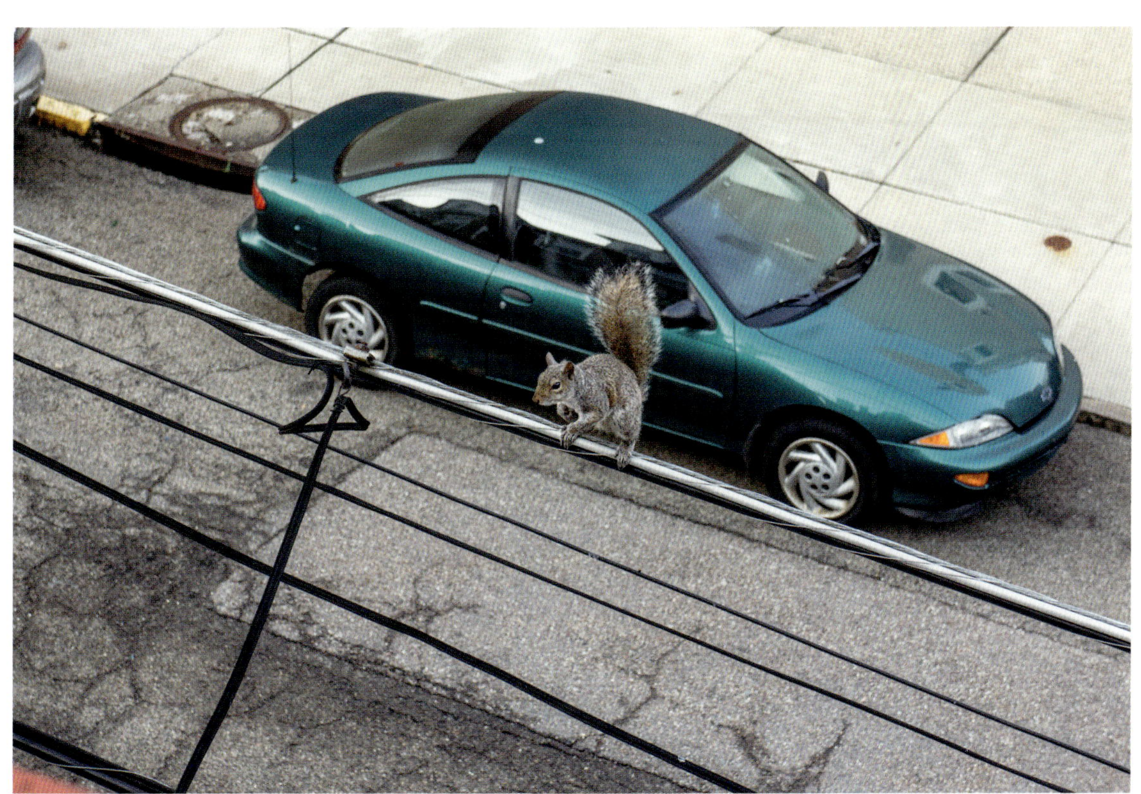

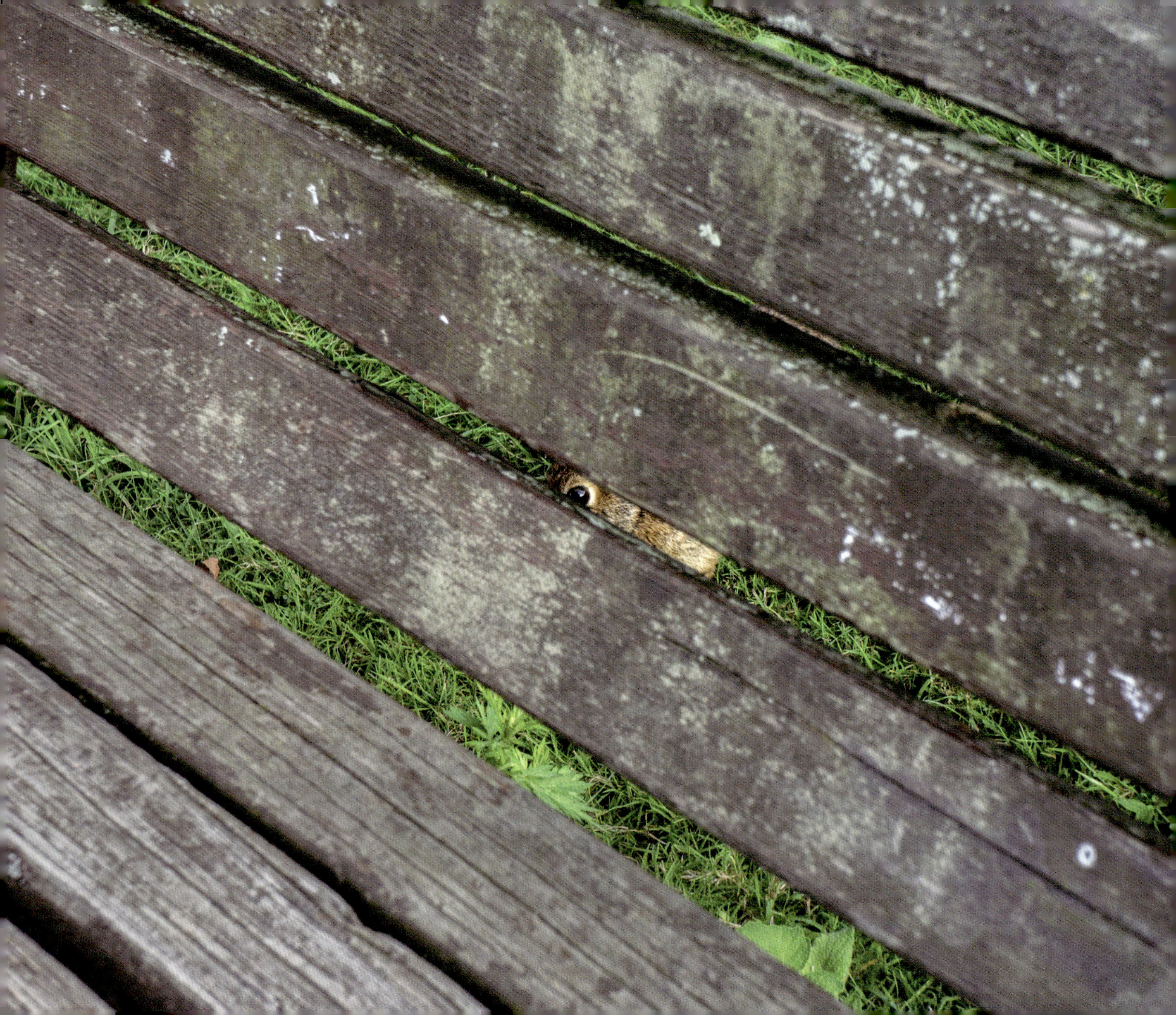

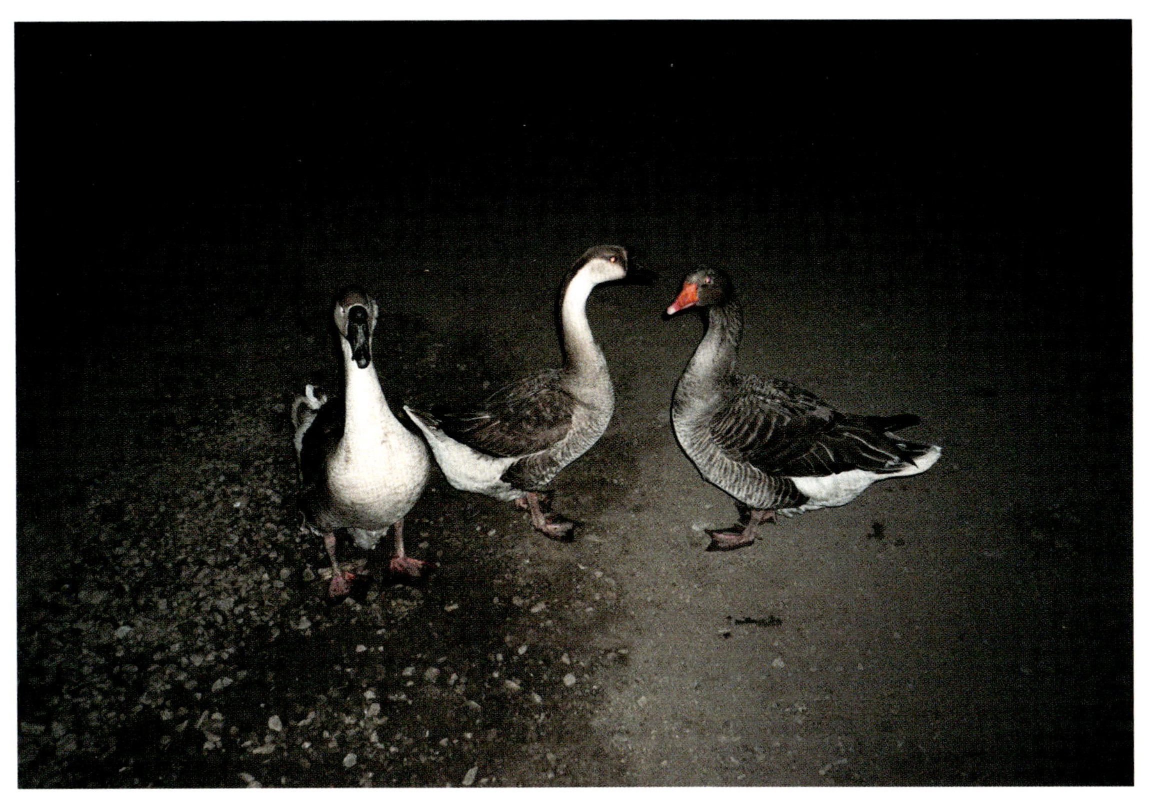

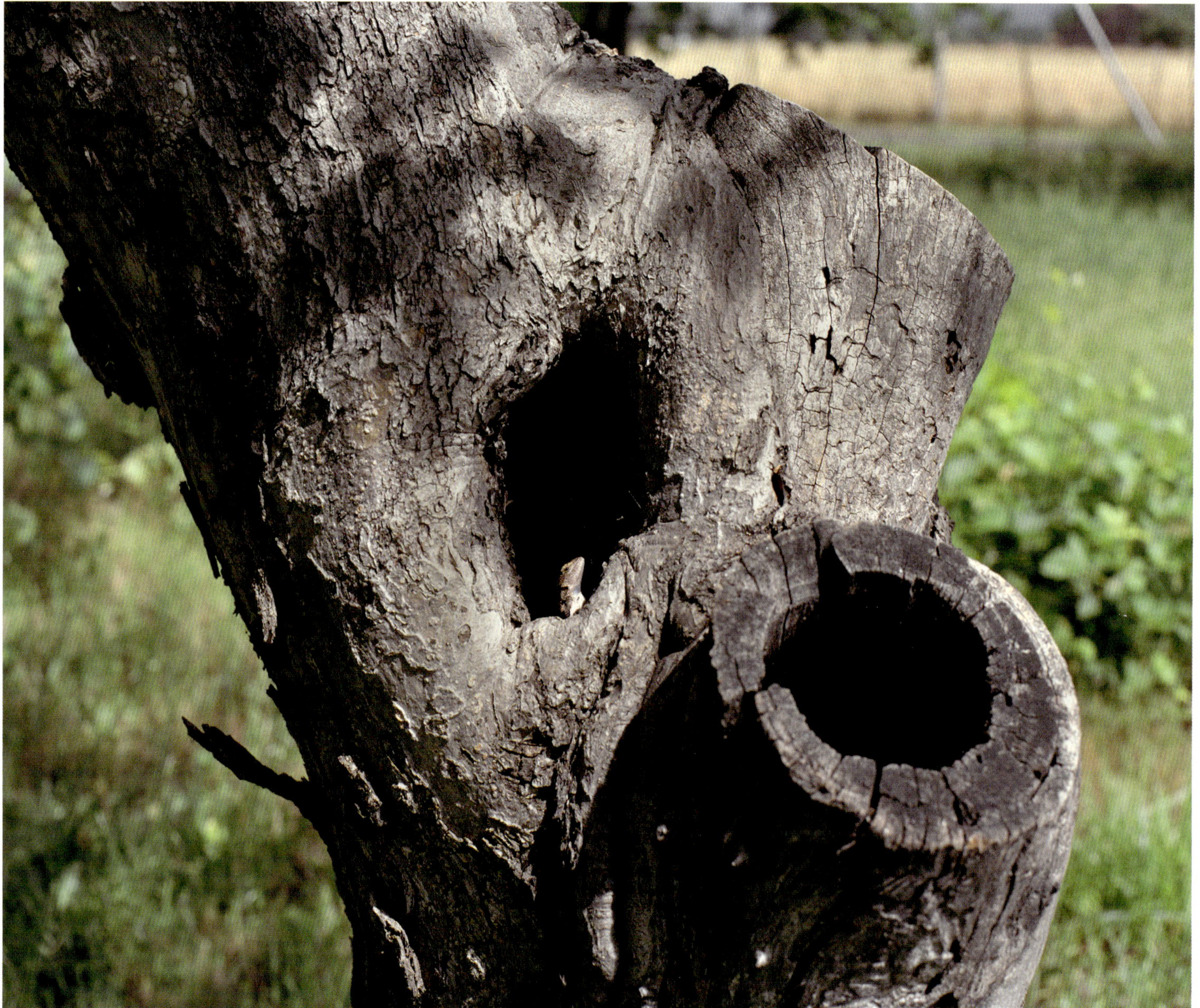

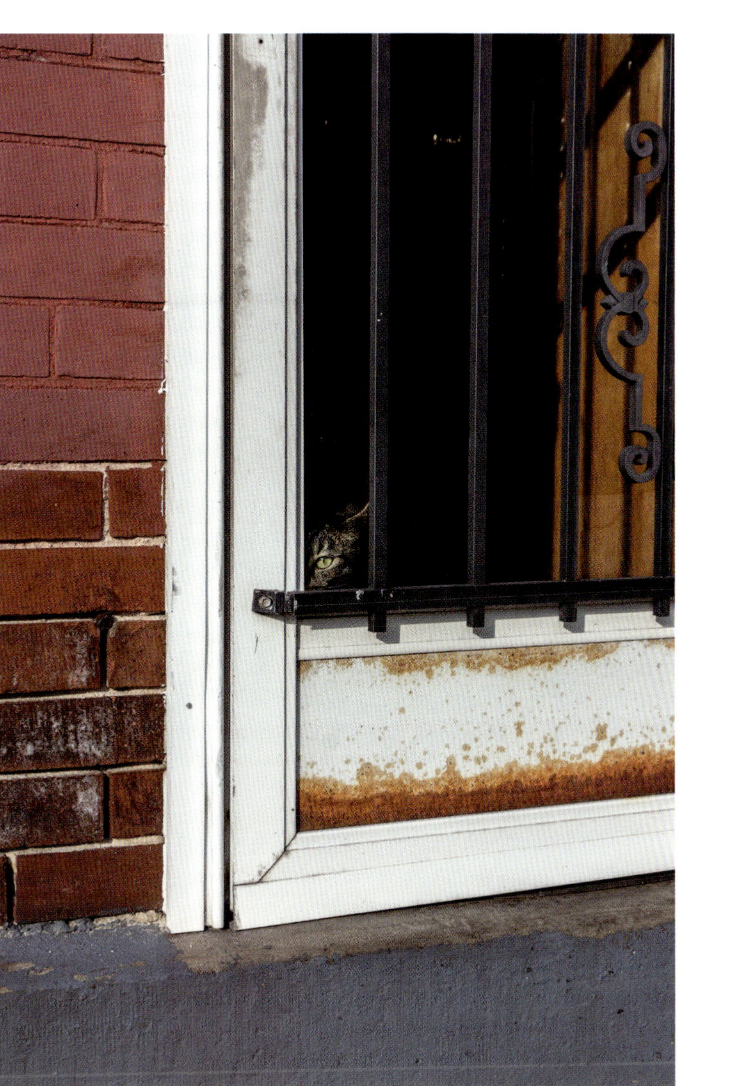

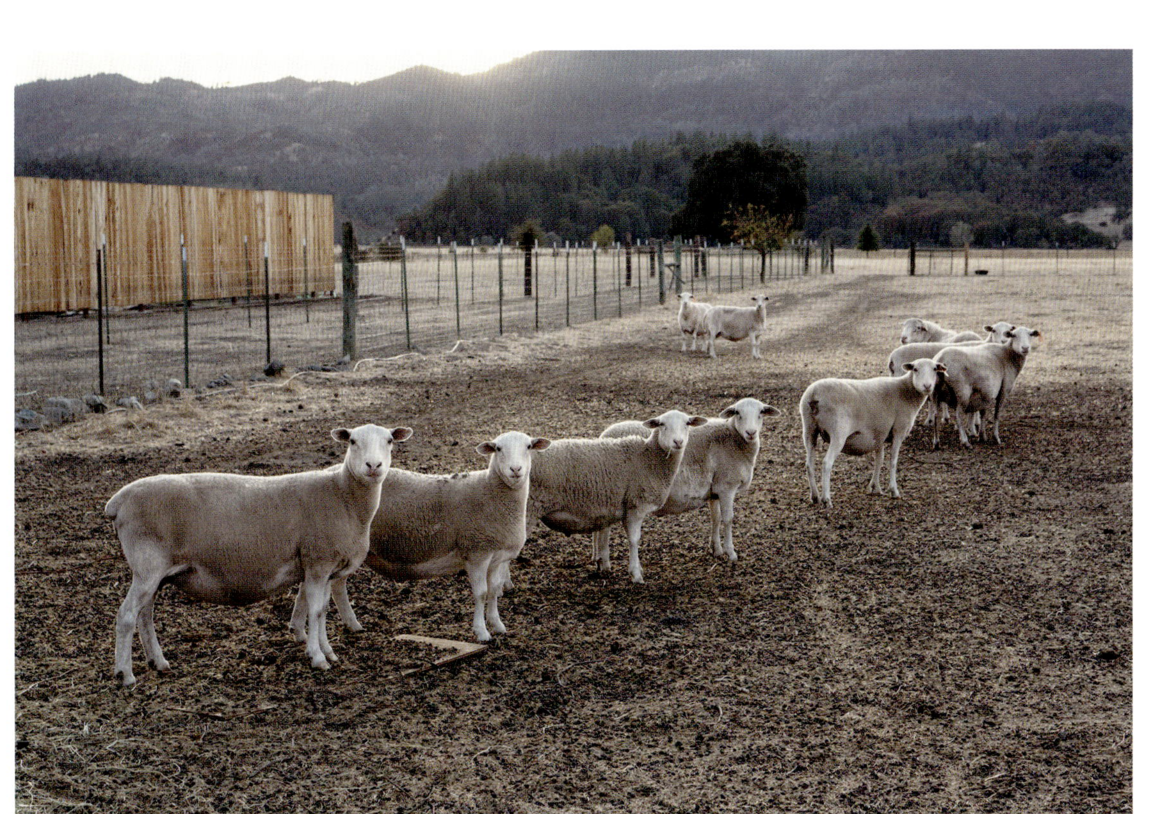

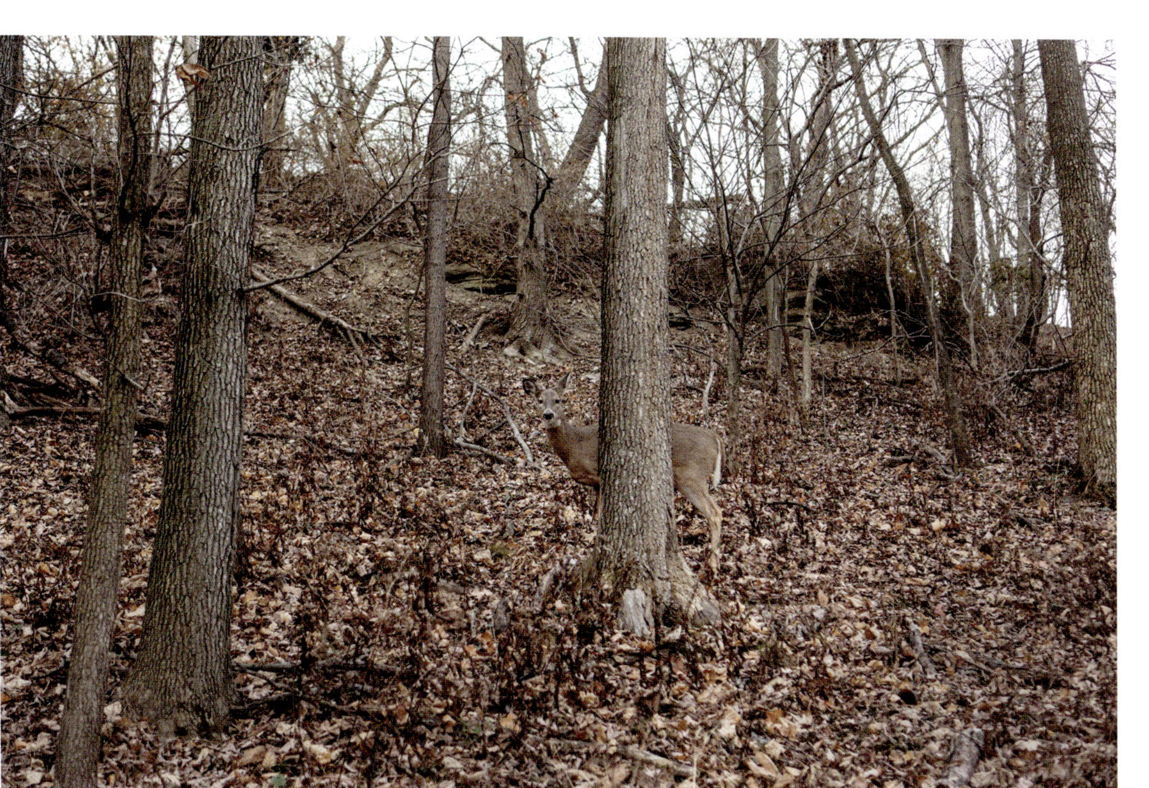

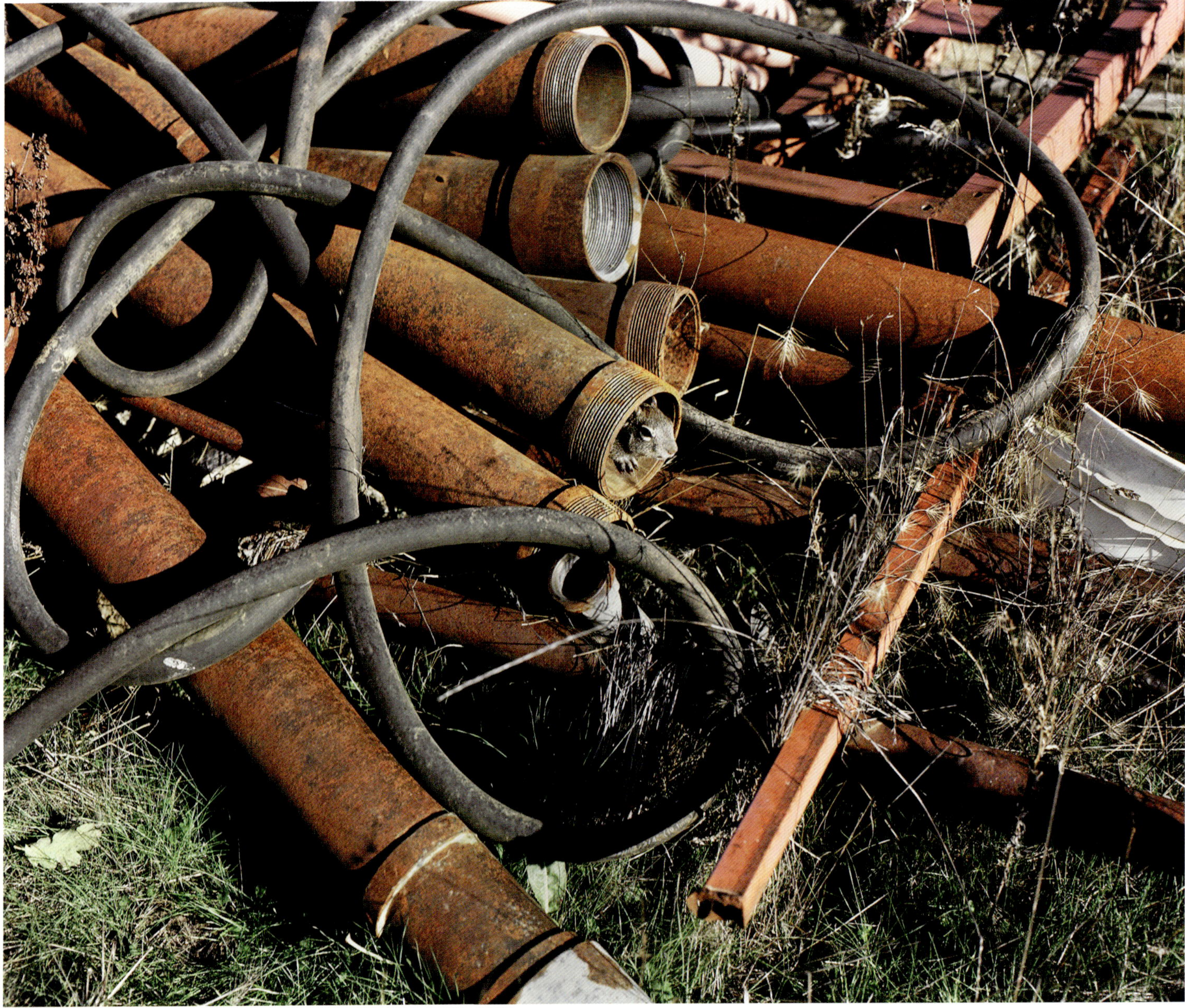

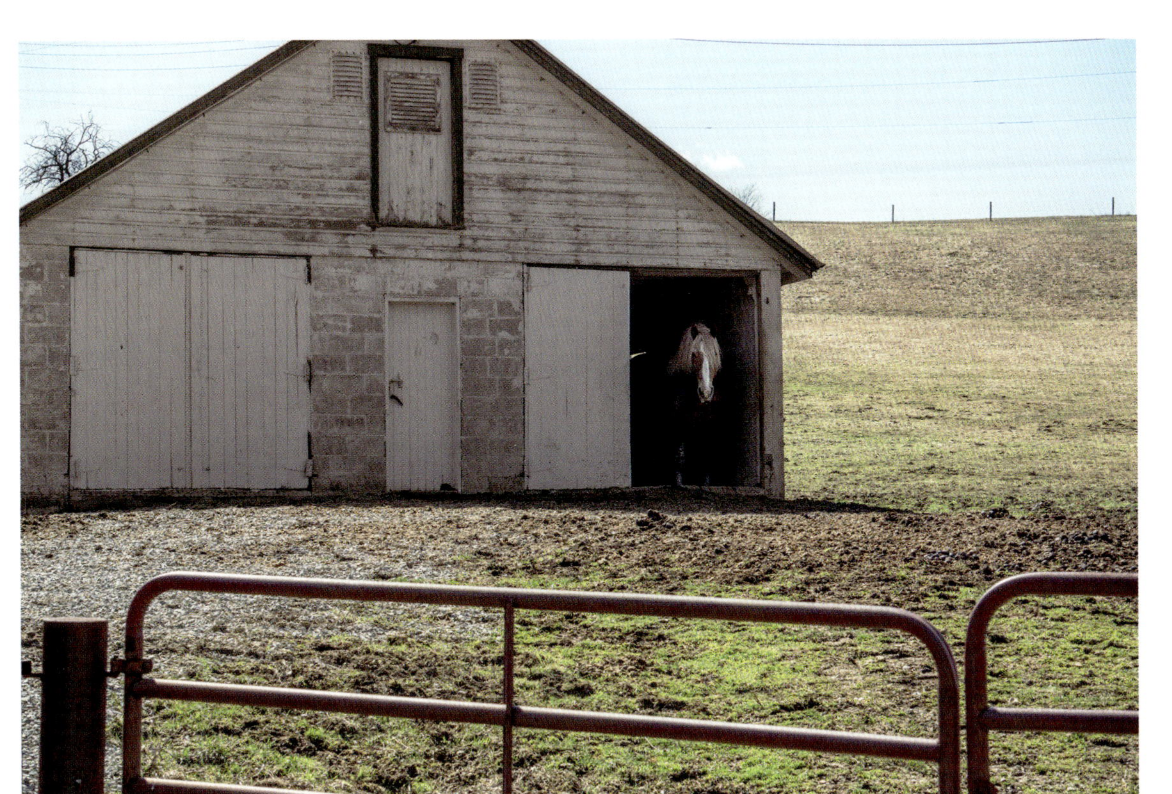

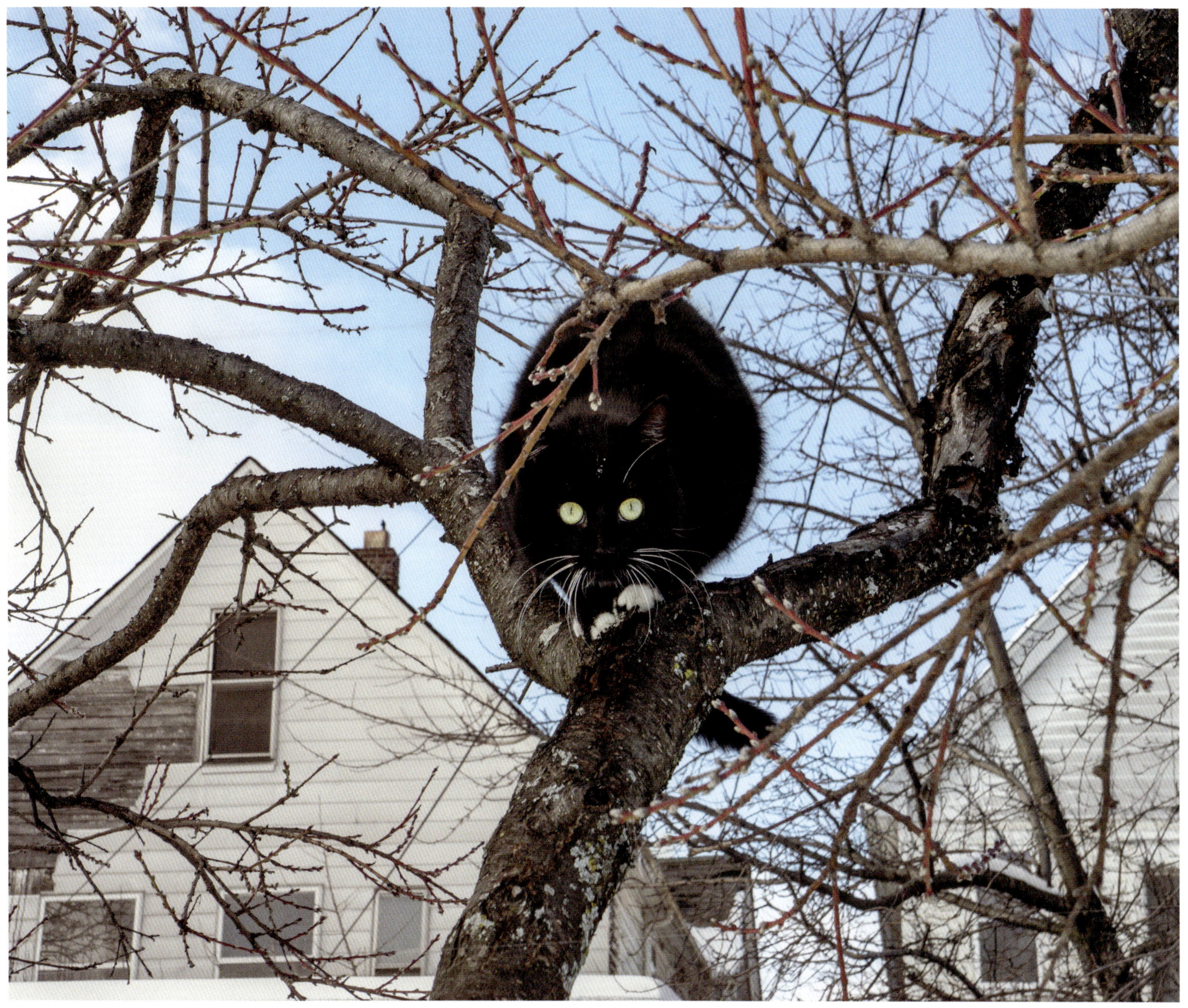

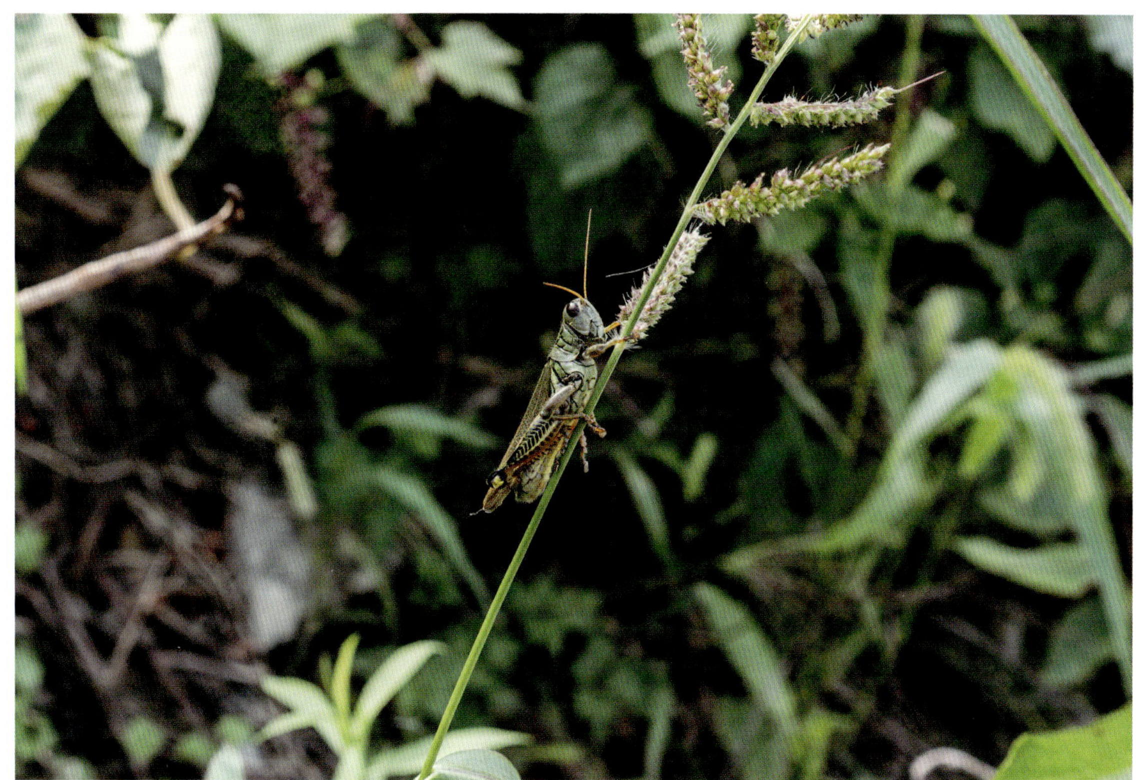

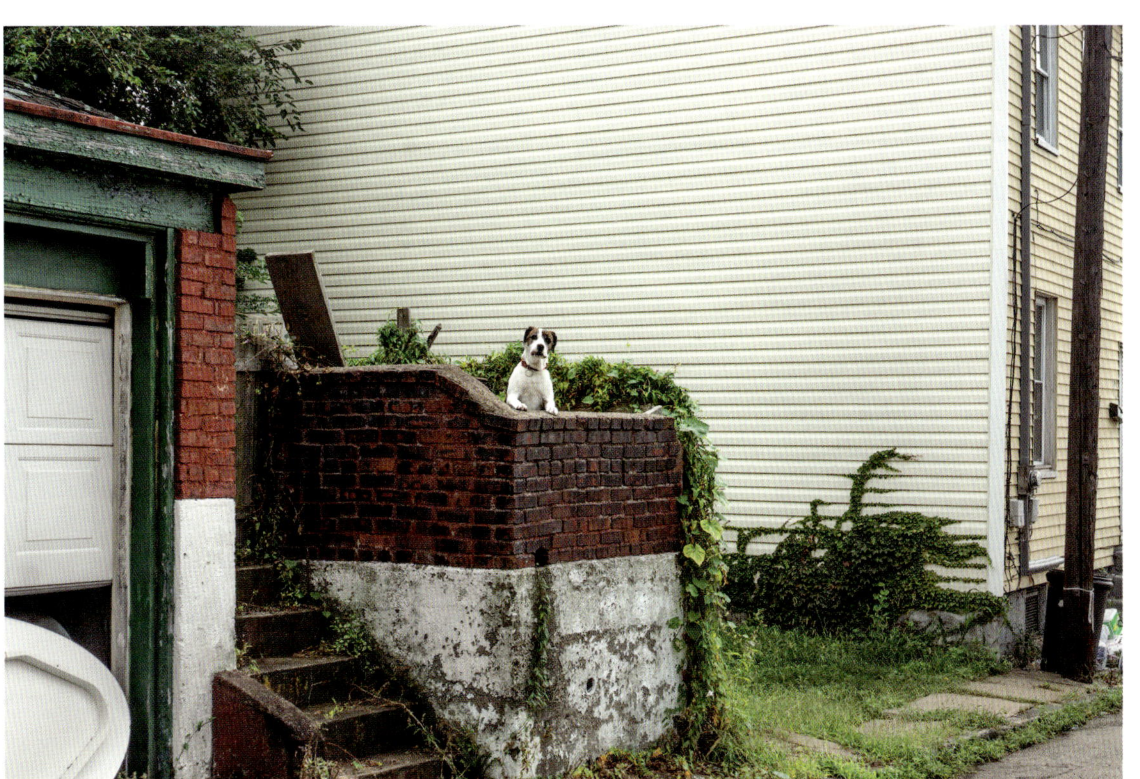

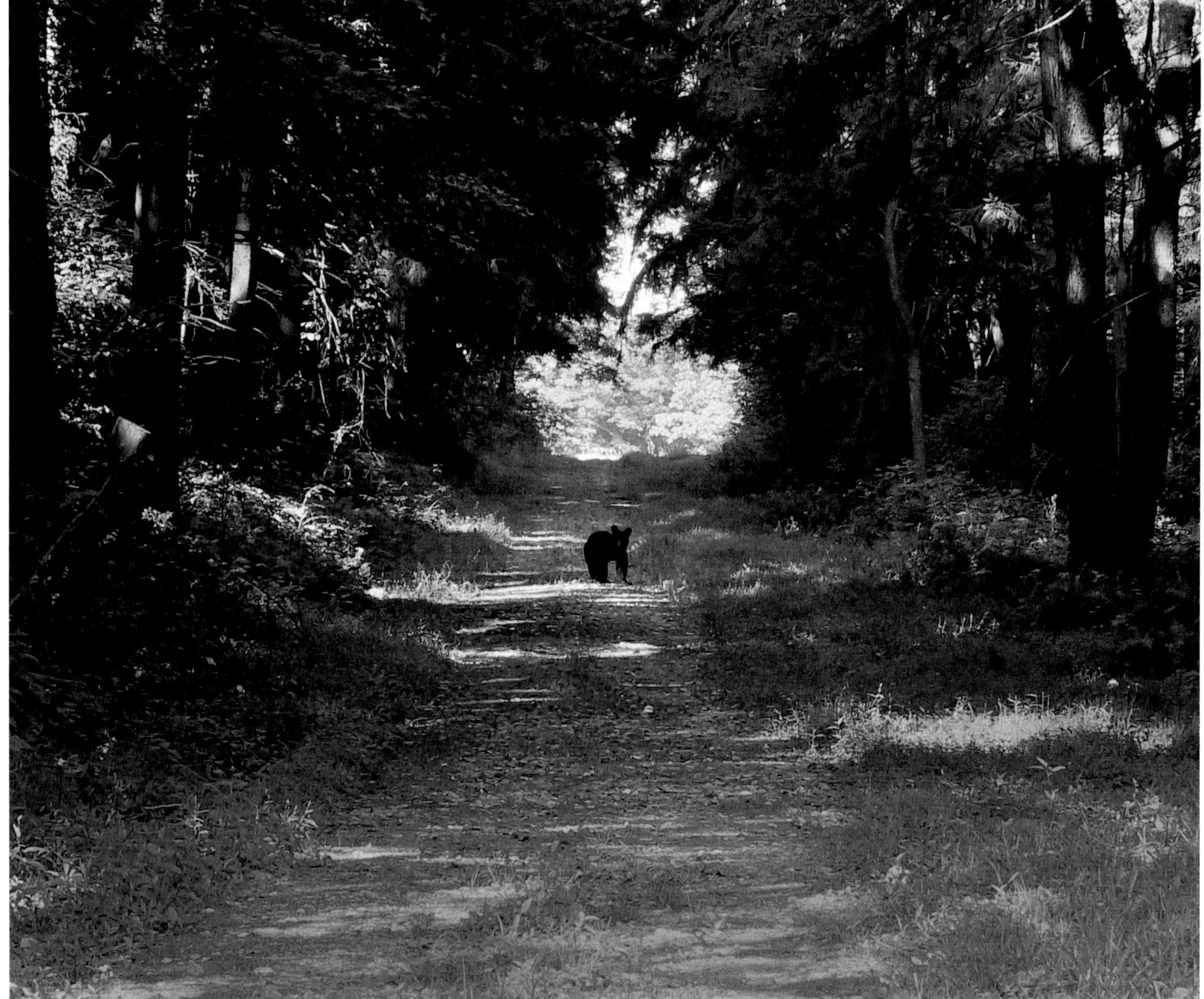

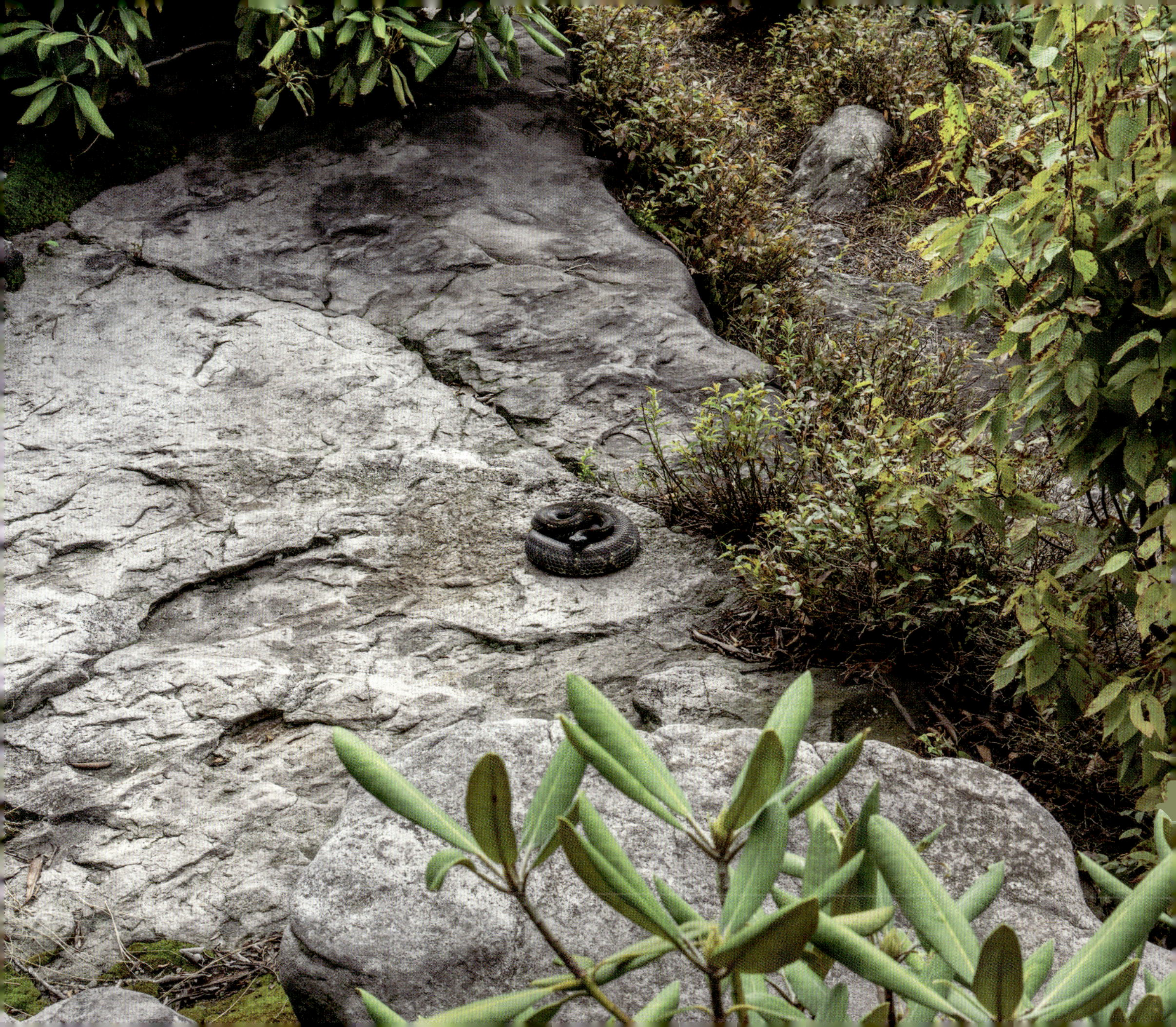

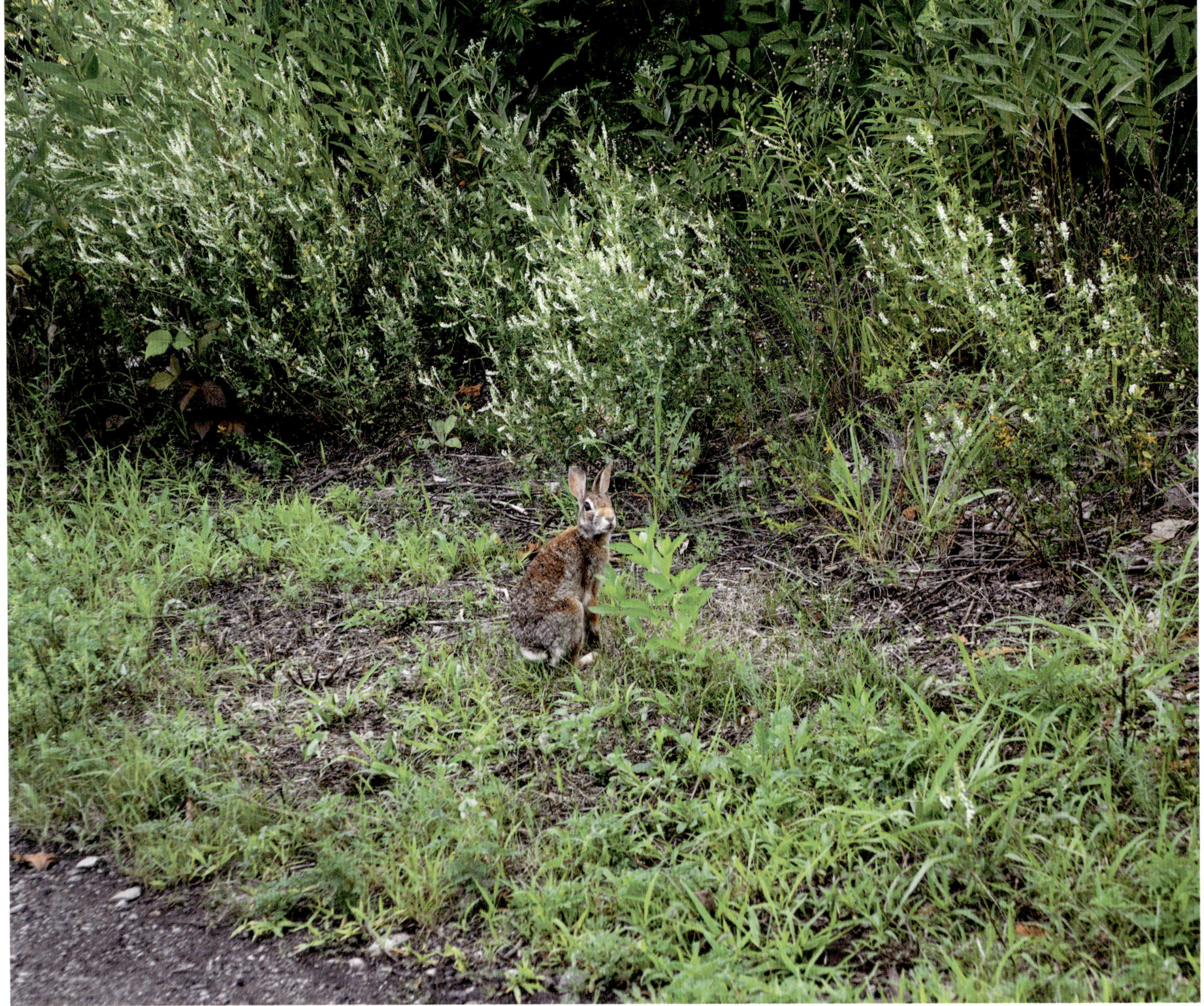

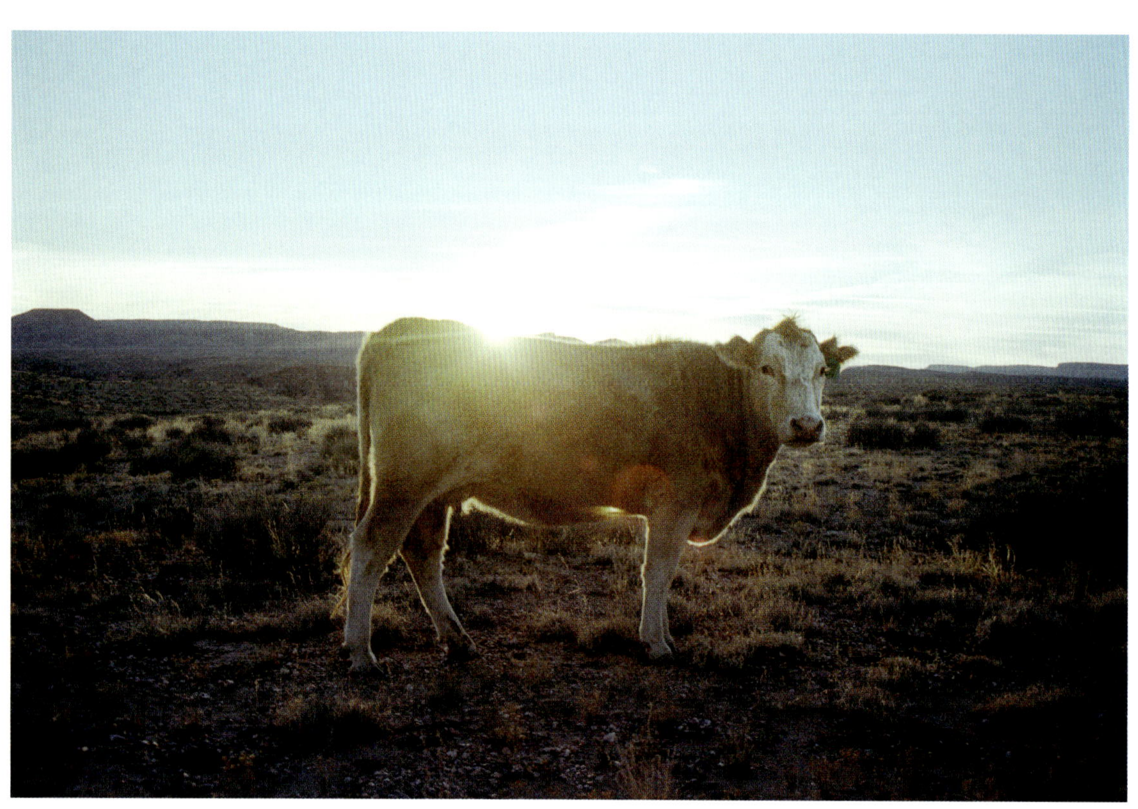

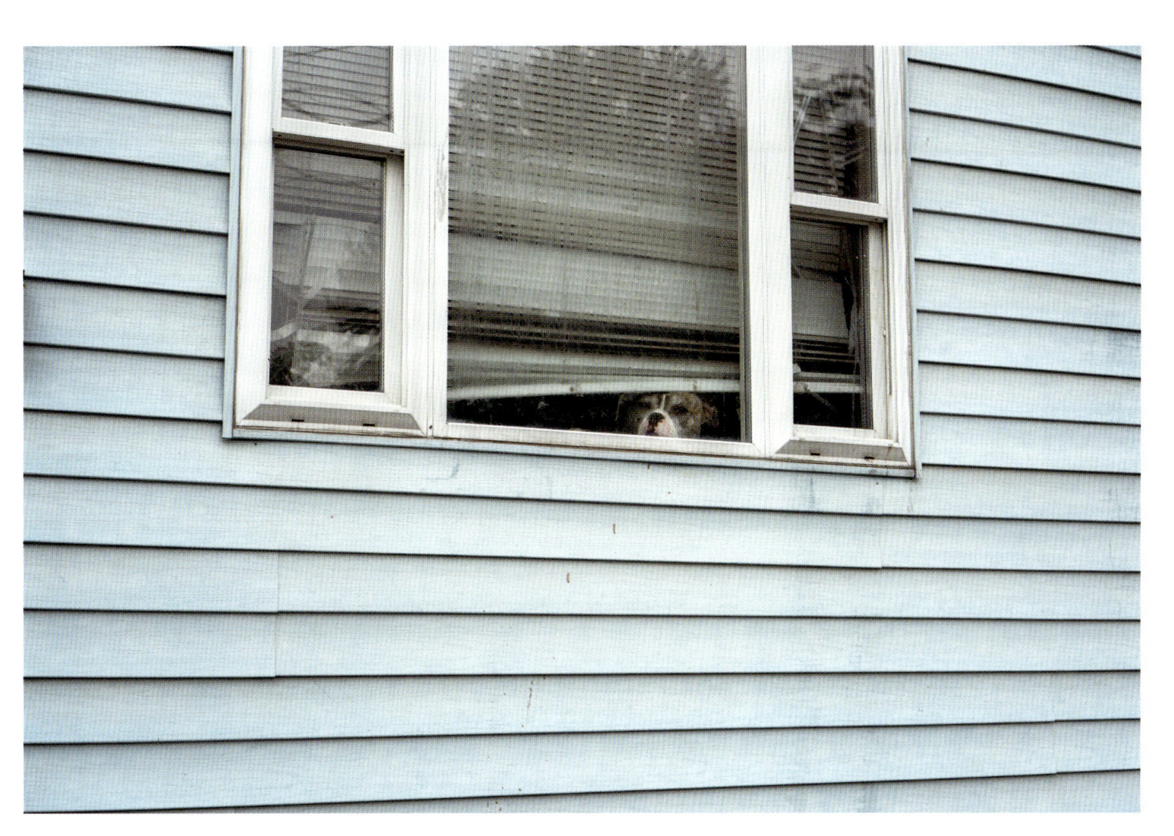

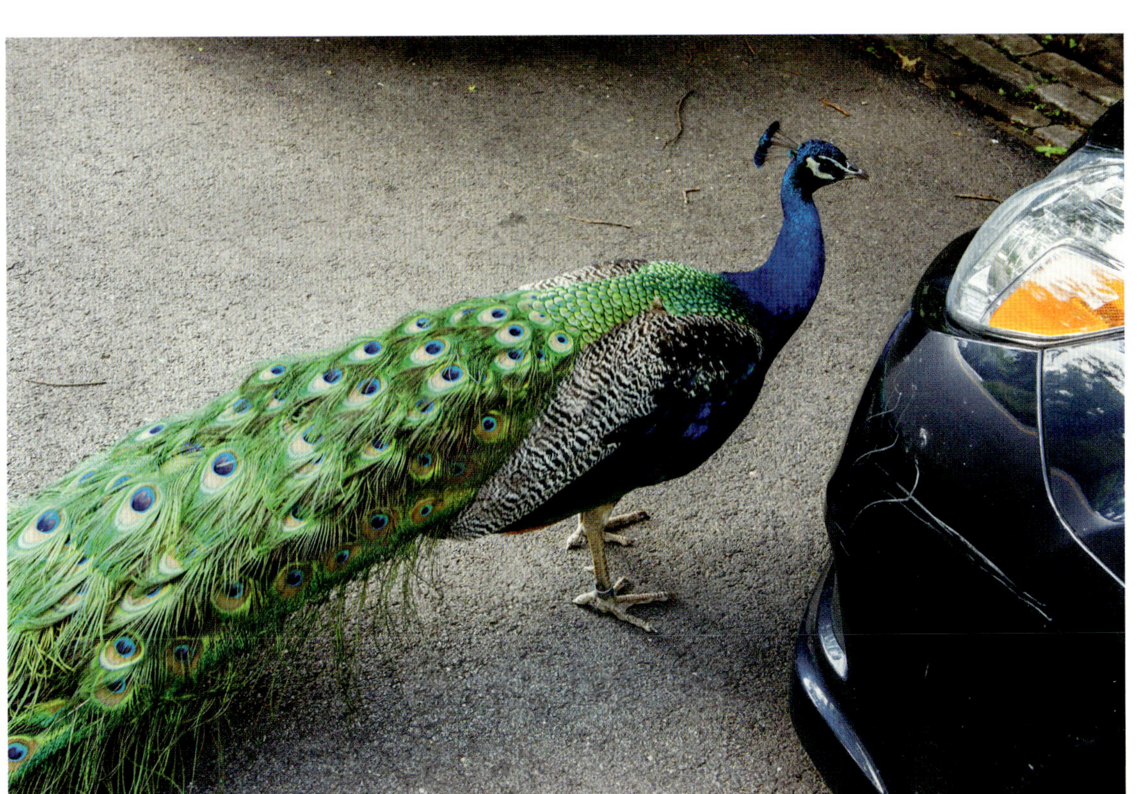

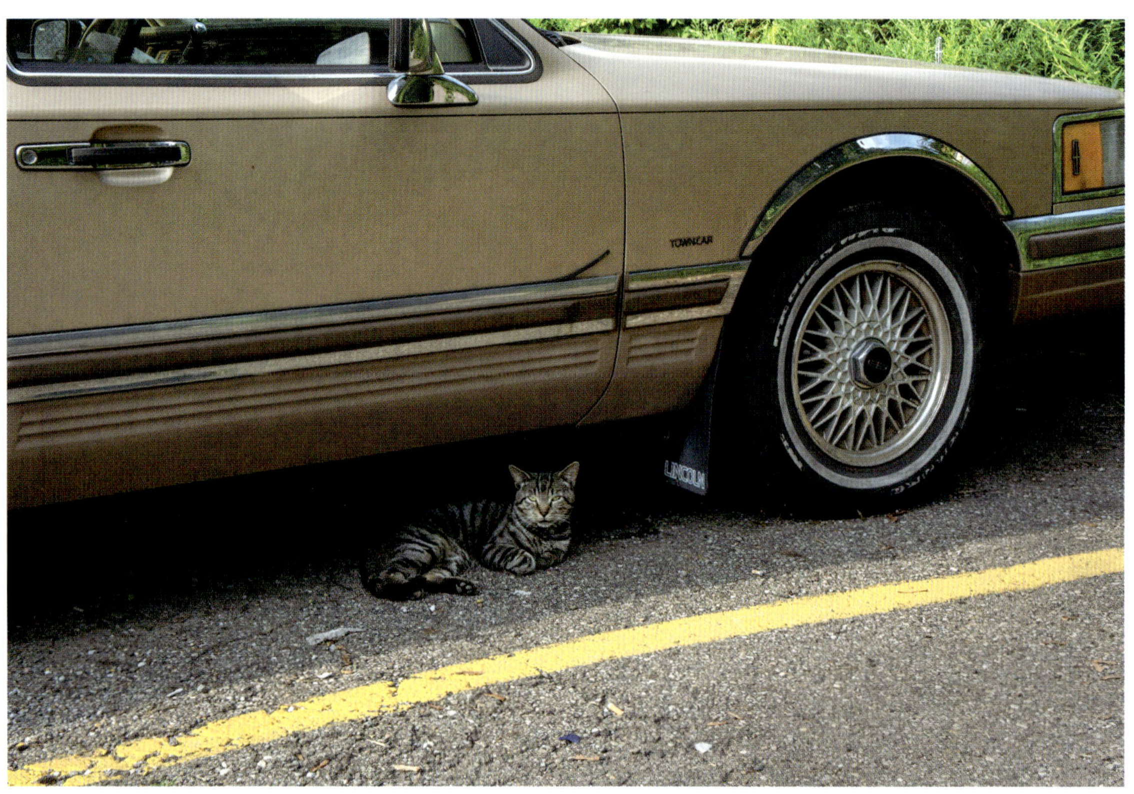
TOWNCAR
LINCOLN

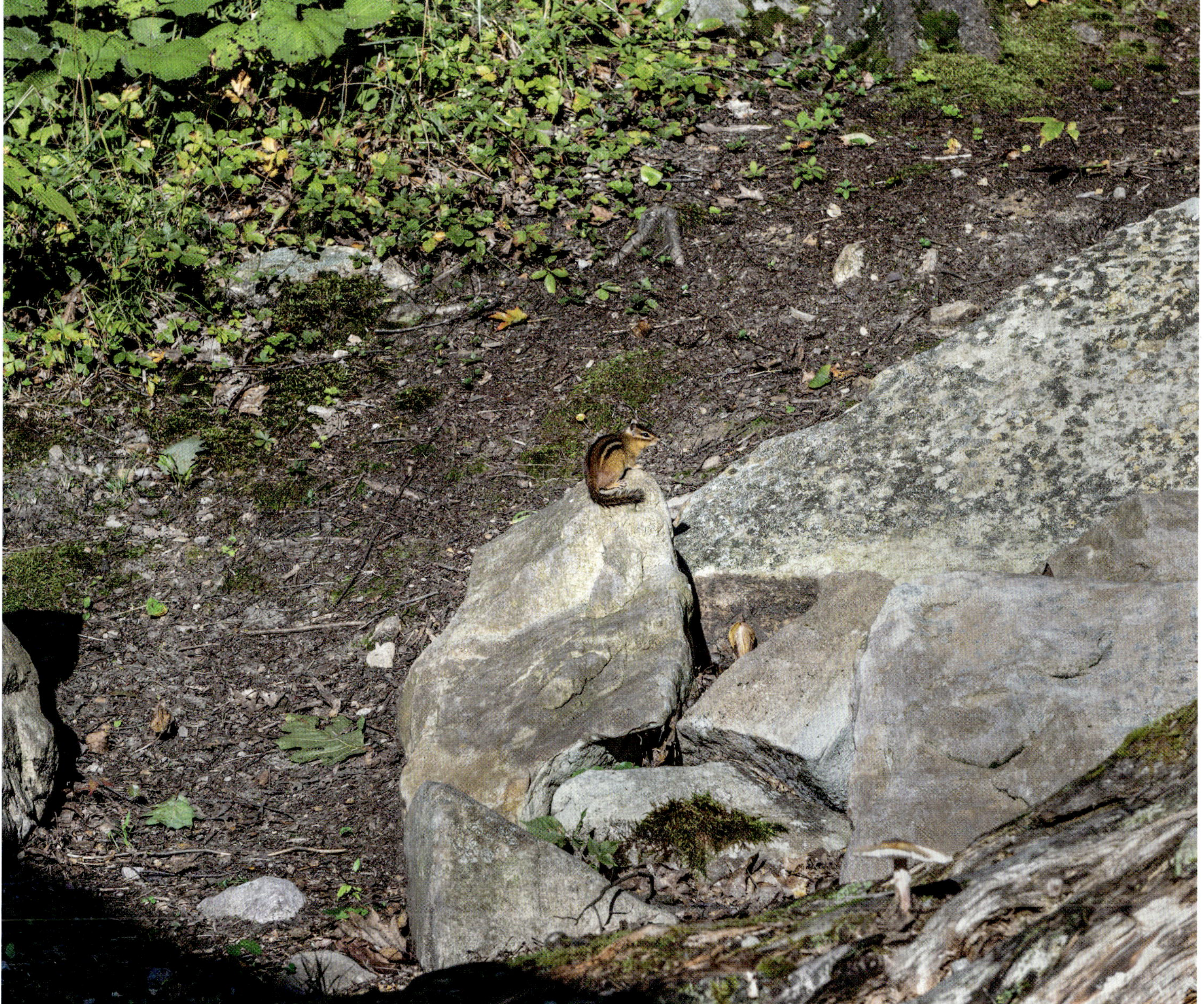

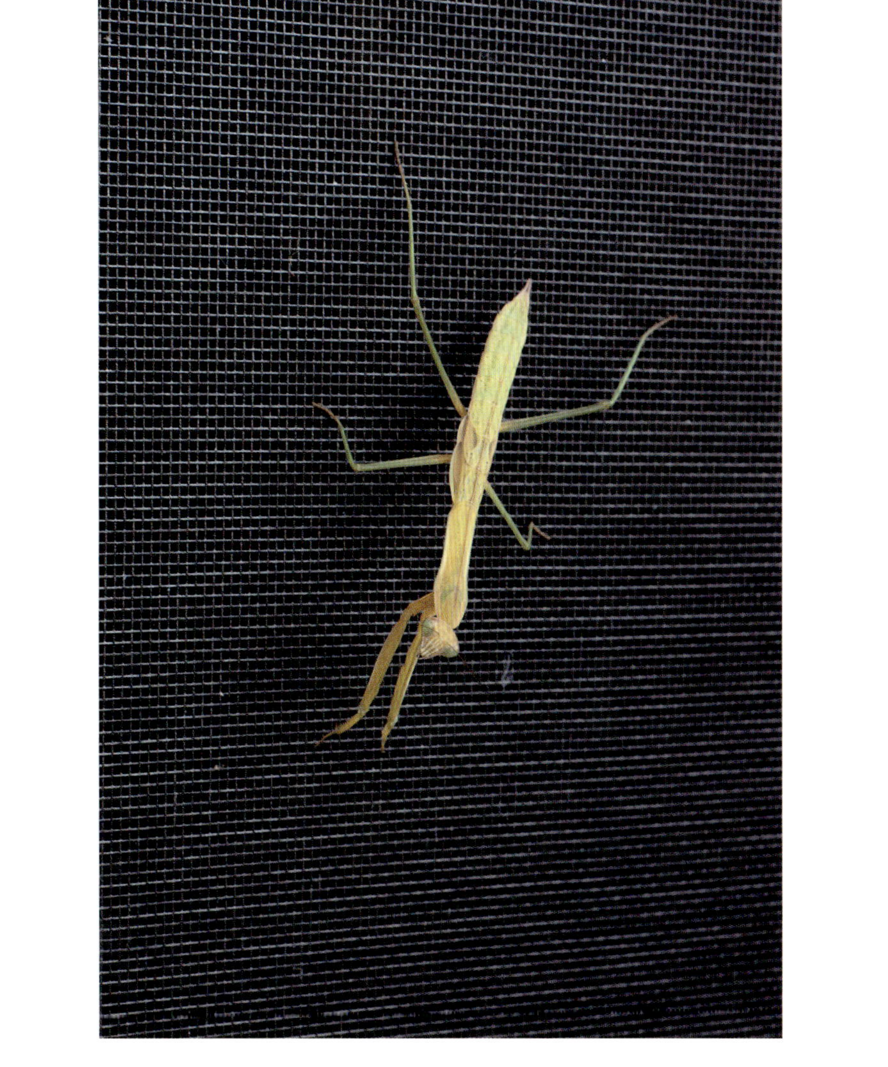

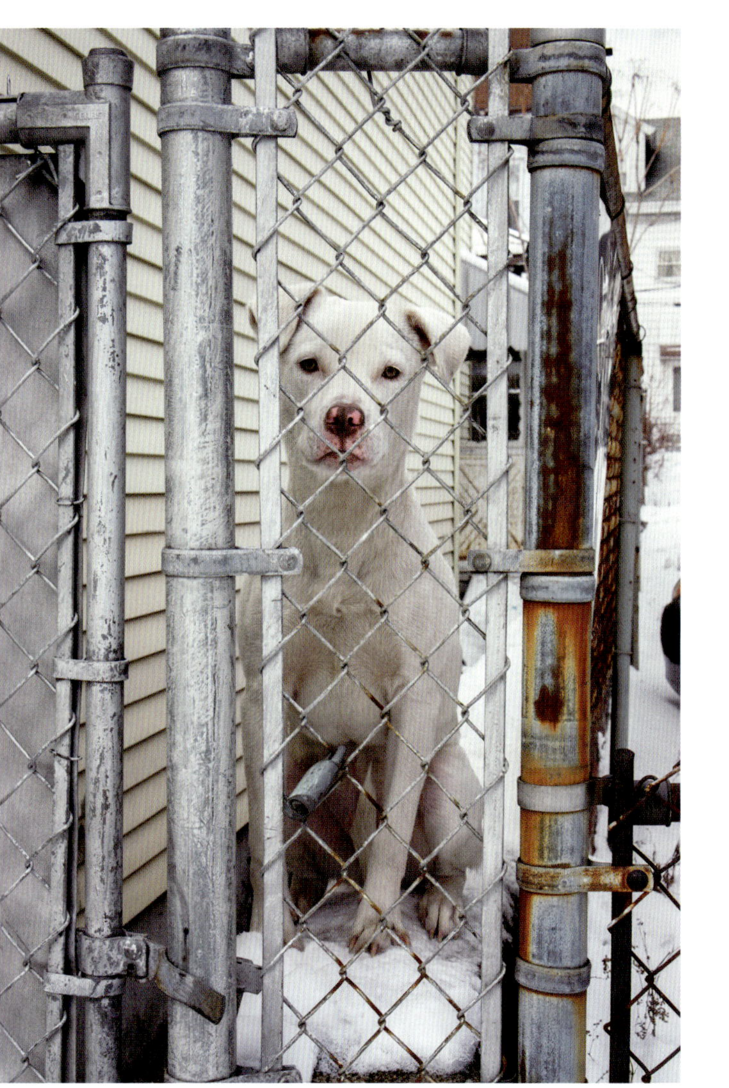

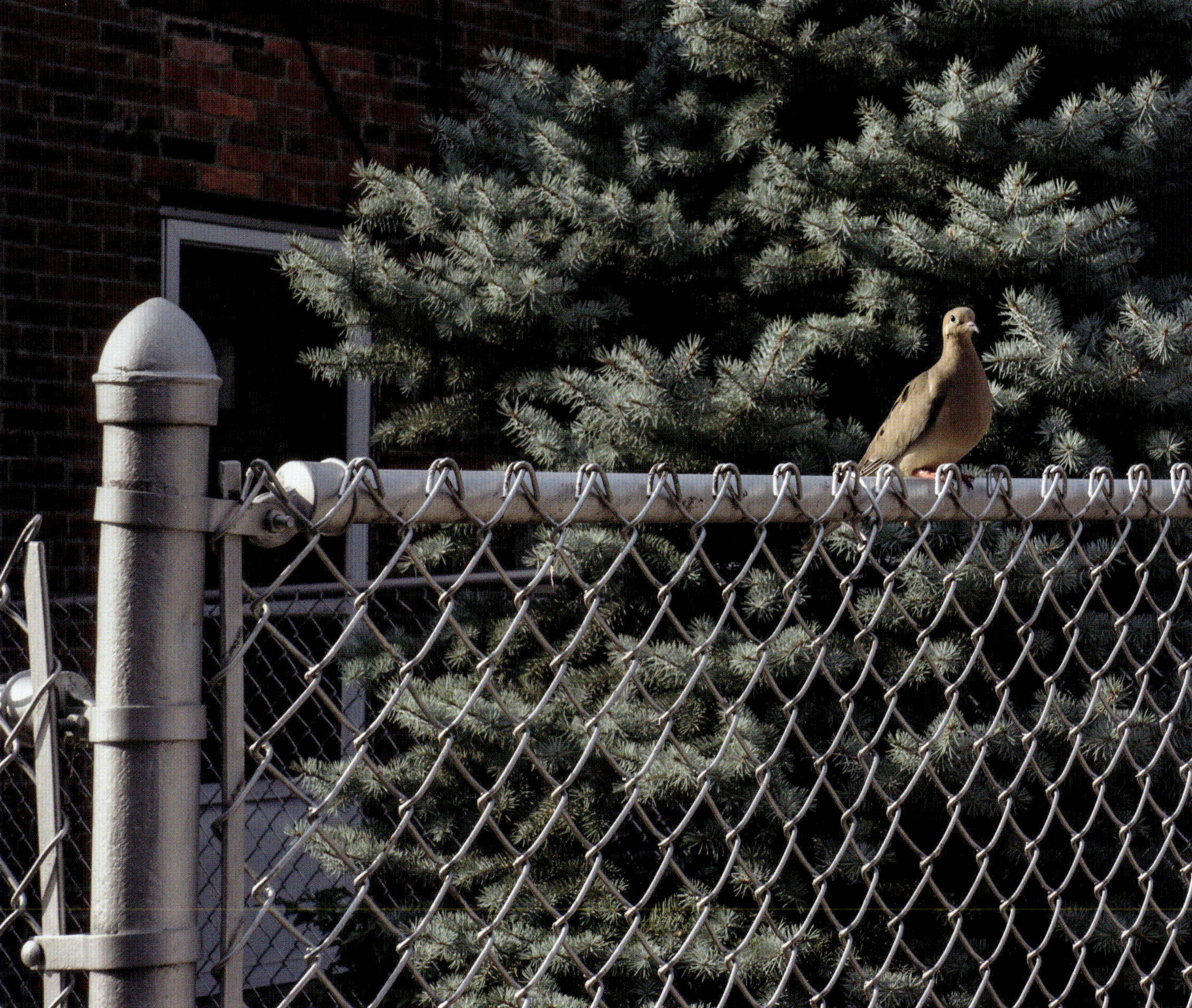

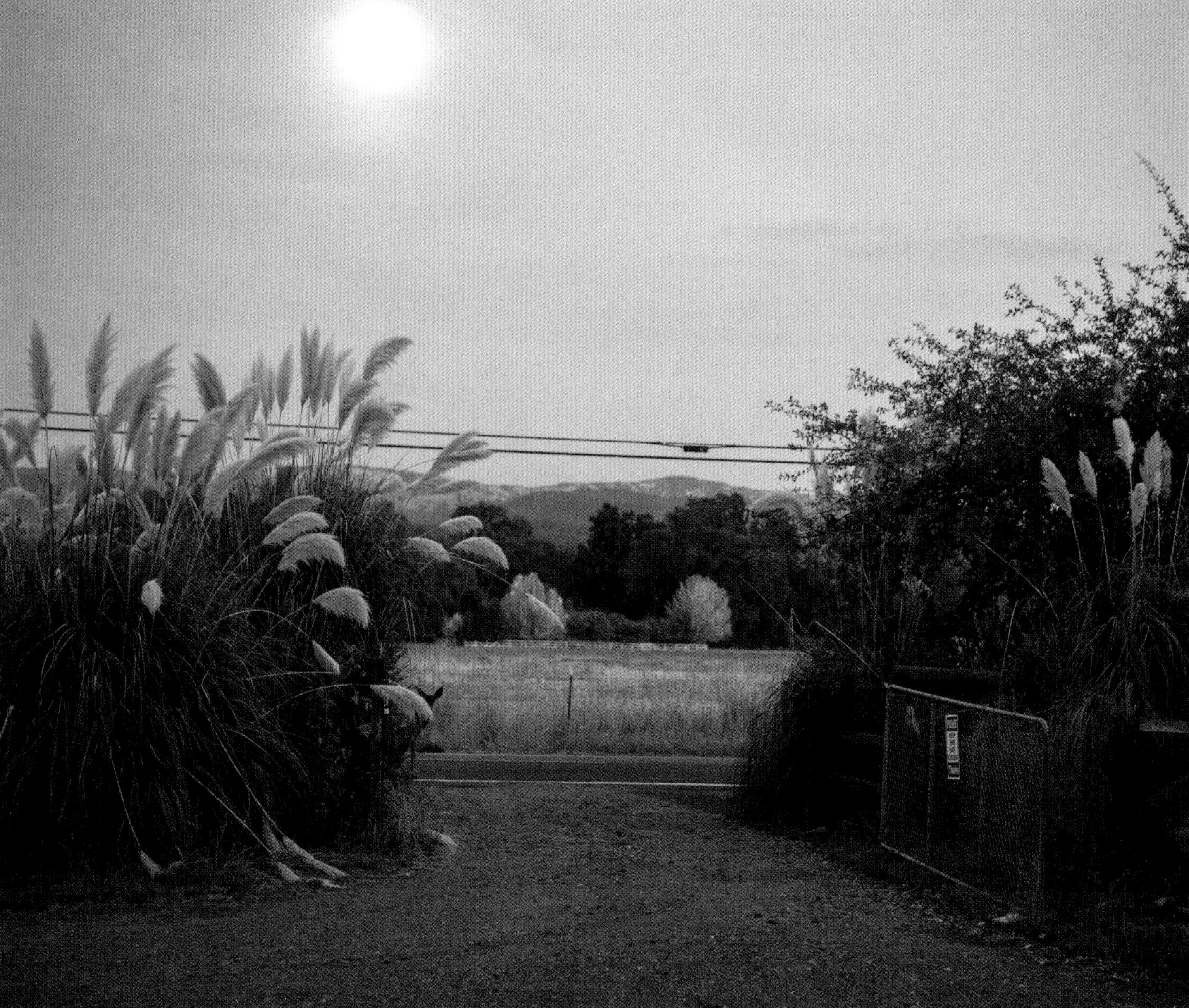

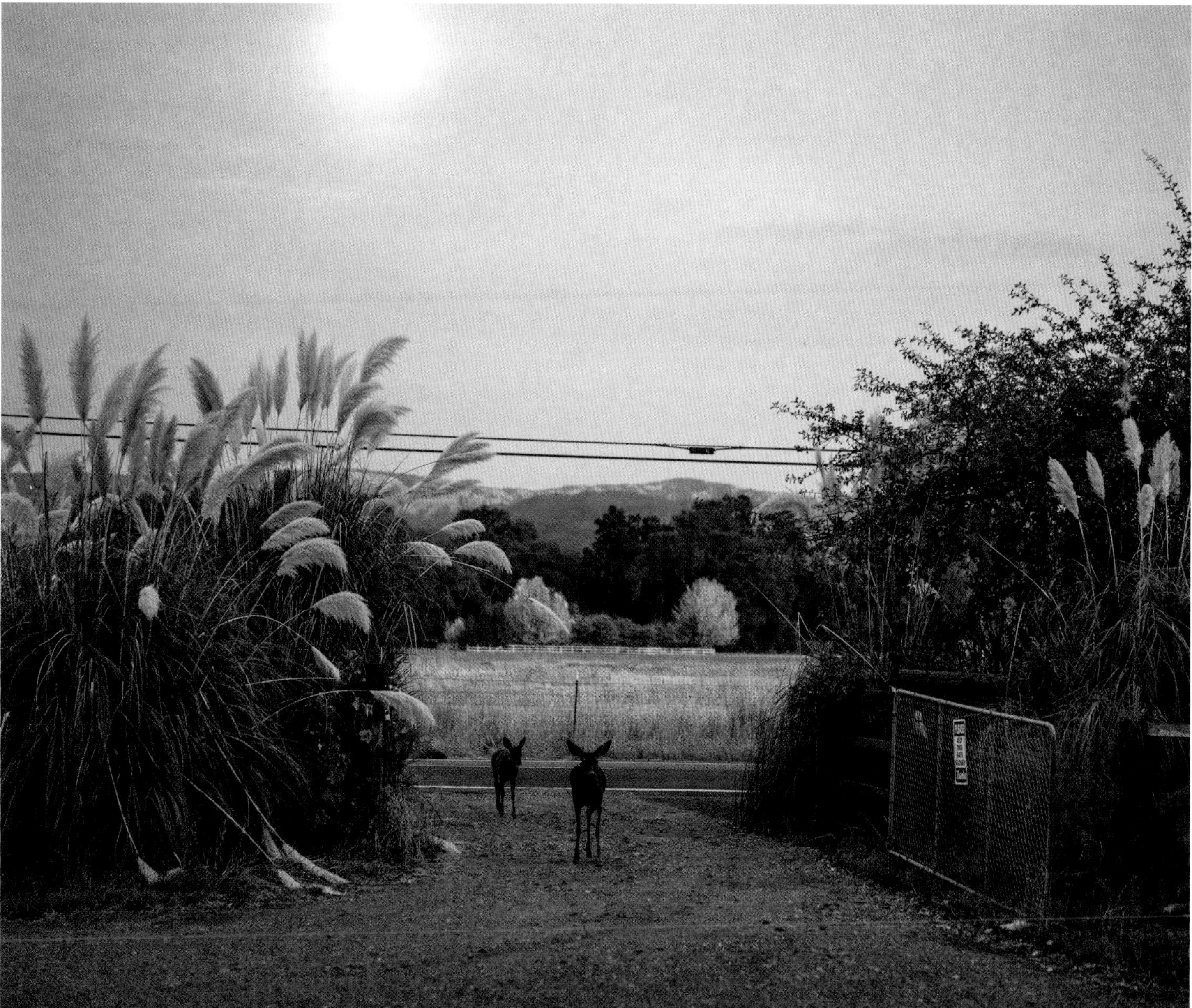

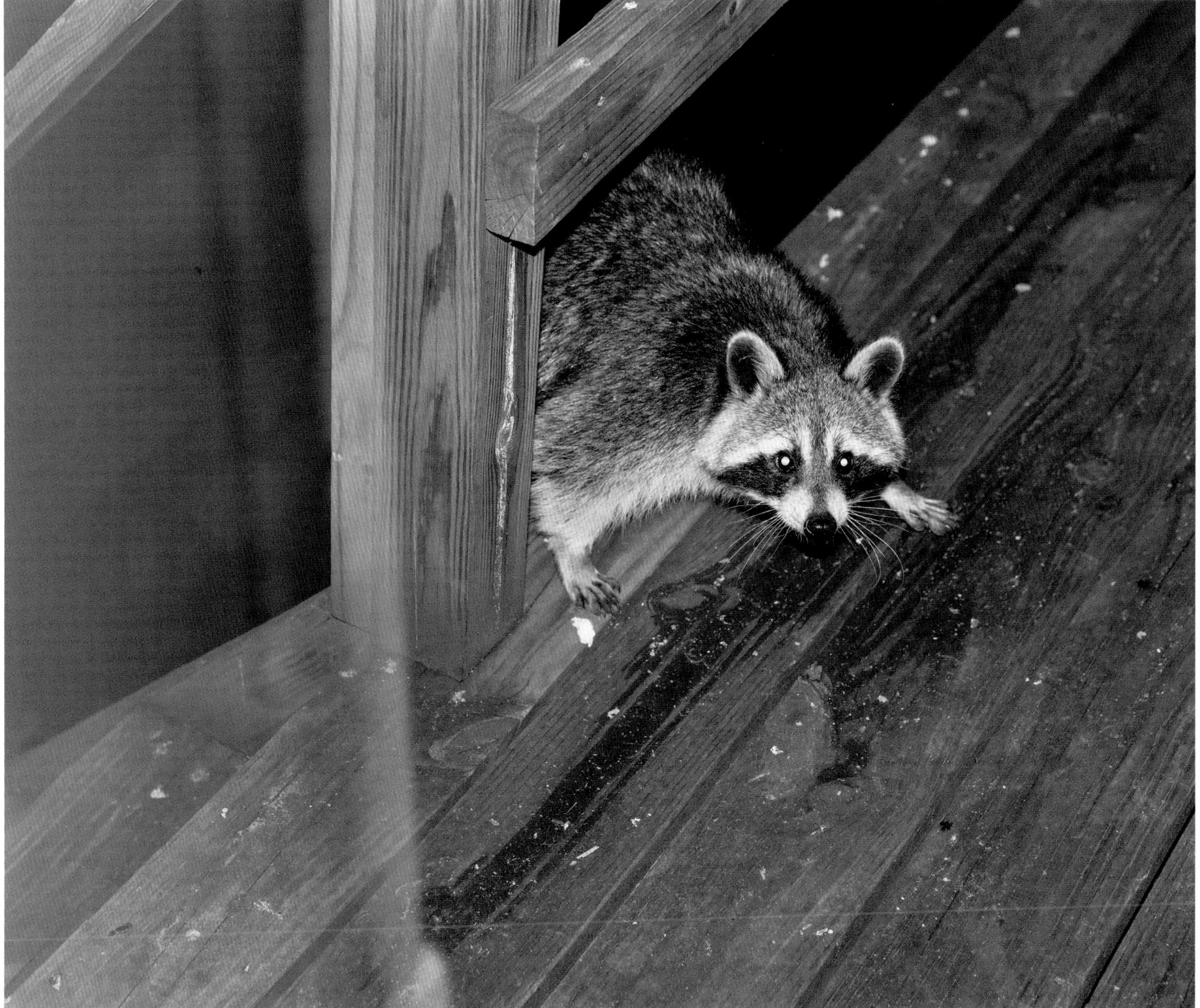

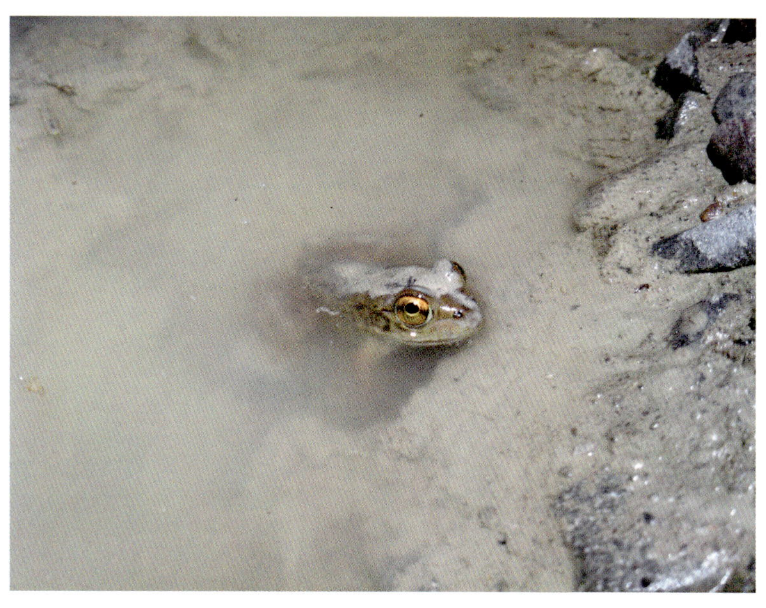

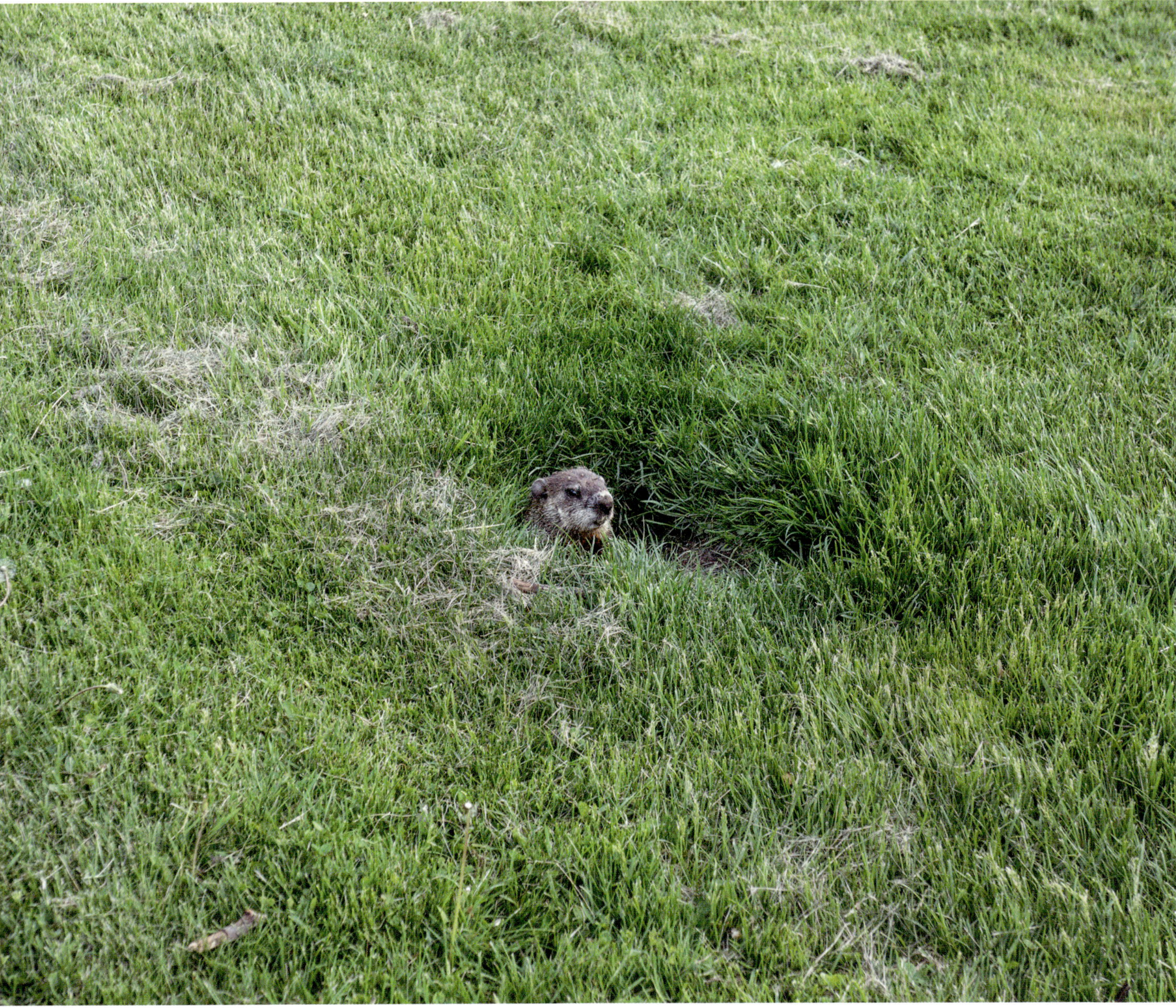

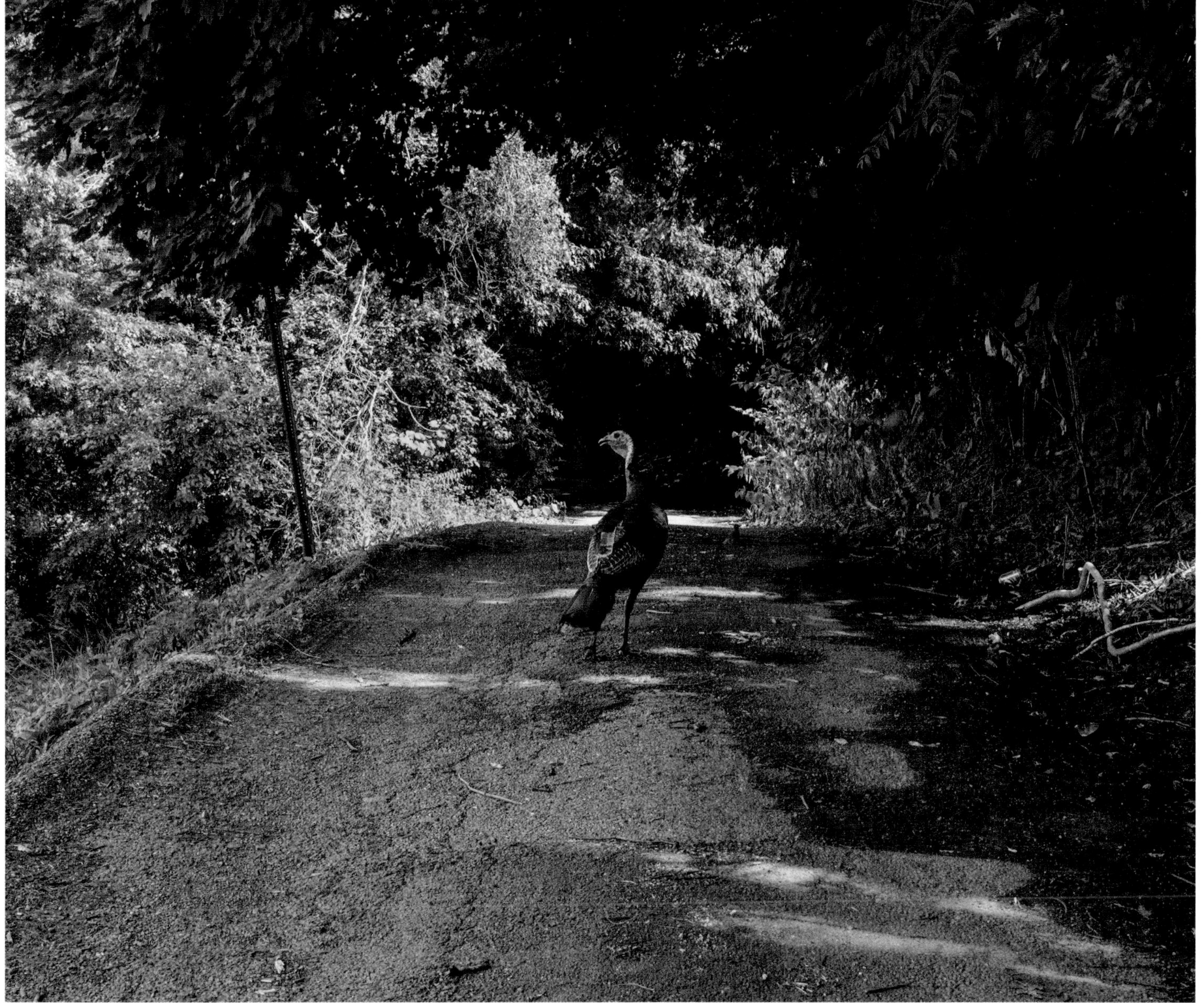

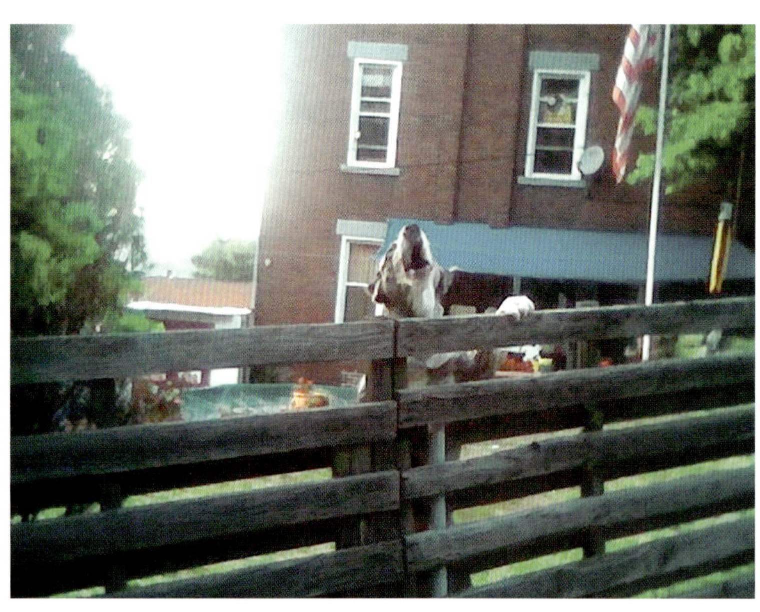

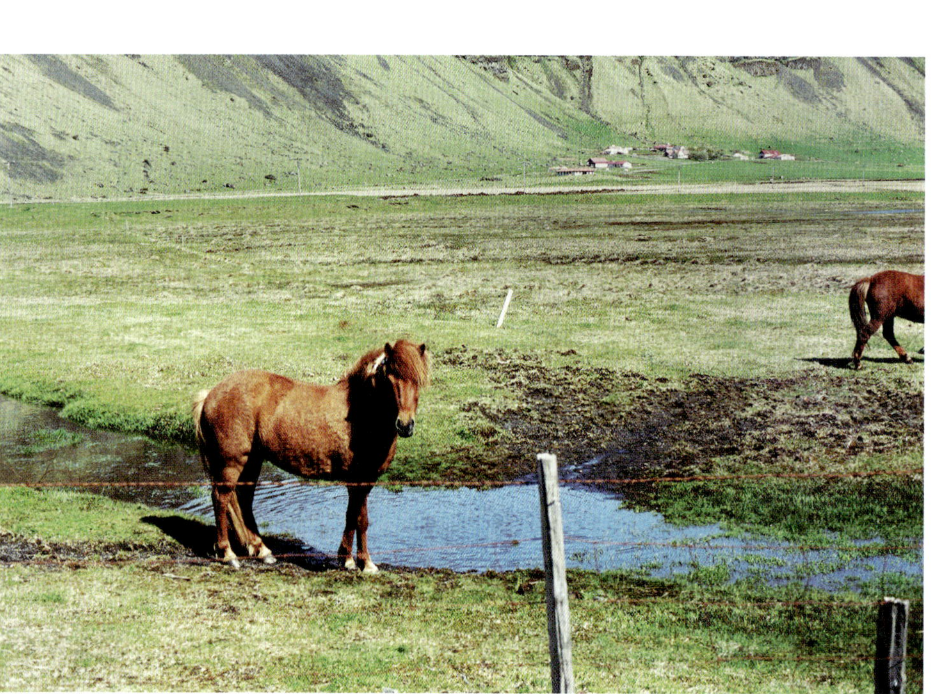

Timothy Morton

BEING SEEN

IF YOU HAVE SUFFERED from trauma, one of the most healing things that can happen to you is *being seen*. Being seen doesn't have to mean that someone actually lays their eyes on you, although that certainly helps. Being seen means that your being is held by the other person without comment, without praise or blame or indifference, just with some kind of open care. One of the most moving parts of the corny blockbuster *Avatar* is the moment at the end when Neytiri, the alien humanoid (albeit blue with a tail), holds in her arms the nearly-dead Jake (whose Na'vi avatar is bonded with her), and as he begins to breathe the oxygen in the mask she has slipped over his face, she says the phrase, which in Na'vi we have been told, early on in the film, means just this unconditional compassionate holding: *I see you.*

Can nonhumans care? Of course they can. Can we?

Why do we assume that it's only us who does the looking? This has to do with the very long history of anthropocentrism, in particular a certain special mode of anthropocentrism that developed during the Neolithic age, the age we also call the agricultural age, marked by the settling down of humans in static dwellings surrounded by farms in places such as Mesopotamia, parts of what is now China, Africa and the Americas. This is the age in which we find ourselves, when we consider the big picture. We are all Mesopotamians. We now live in Mesopotamia 9.0, which is called neoliberal capitalism. Mesopotamia keeps upgrading because it keeps crashing. The logistics of Neolithic agriculture—I call it *agrilogistics*—are such that it is bound to create deserts. The history of so-called "civilization" is from this point of view simply the history of the endless retreats of agrilogistics from the deserts it has created.

Way before philosophy formalized the anthropocentric depersonalization of animals, agrilogistics was busy beginning to hardwire it into social space. Start with a field that demarcates a place called Nature beyond the human realm. Begin to call the nonhumans in that realm cattle—patriarchy being what it is, dehumanized women also fell into this category frequently in most versions of Mesopotamia. Suspect the cats who show up on the boundary, refuting by their very presence—and their handy way of catching the rats that ate the corn in the house that Jack built—the supposed rigid, thin qualities of this boundary. Suspect them and turn them into gods, or demonic familiars, or aliens (why do they have cat eyes? Because cats are the *intraterrestrial alien*).

But this setting up of an absurd boundary—absurd because not in accord with the symbiotic real—also begins to happen in human psychic space. Let's start calling this what it is. Let's start calling it The Severing. We keep on and on retraumatizing ourselves by reasserting, like someone with Stockholm syndrome siding with her or his captors (ourselves), that we are humans and we don't need anyone else. The very repetition is a PTSD symptom. Because this is indeed trauma, dear readers. We have cut the ties to the lifeforms that sustain us in social, psychic and philosophical space. Can a cat commit suicide? Why no, opines the commenter in a random article I found in *New Scientist*, grief-stricken that my cat had been run over, and knowing how upset he seemed the days and weeks beforehand. Why can't a cat commit suicide? Because to do that you need a self-concept, and it's evident (is it not?) that cats have no self-concept.

The zombie meme is everywhere. Humans *act*. The beings we violently call "animals" just *behave*. Chimps can't be rescued from zoos because chimps aren't people, so chimps aren't ever in prison, because to be in prison (suffering in confinement) you need to be a person. Humans *imagine*. Even poor Neanderthals weren't able to do that, we told ourselves, until we discovered their DNA intermingled with ours.

And the zombie agrilogistics keeps on churning away, ploughing up the Earth like a battleship cutting through water—the act that already filled Sophocles with uncanny disturbance. We have automated The Severing. Are we ever going to throw our bodies on the gears and stop it?

"Animals" *look*. Humans *see*.

We used to do this in reductionist, atomist mode. Animals are just machines, for instance, and machines can't be people. (We keep insisting on it, despite the paranoia even of Descartes that he might just be an android. Descartes himself, who thought animals were just extensional lumps joined together to make machinery.)

Now we do it in another kind of reductionist mode, called

correlationism. This is the cool kids' philosophy, the going way of thinking about things since the age of Kant. There is a real, but it only becomes reality when something (guess what? Always so far something human) accesses it, rather like there is a light in the refrigerator, but you only get to see whether it's on or not by opening the fridge. Many fridge-openers have been suggested: the transcendental subject (Kant), spirit (Hegel), economic relations (Marx), will to power (Nietzsche), Dasein (Heidegger)...what these all have in common is that you would be right to put the word *human* in front of all of them. Cats can't access things: so cats have no reality. This is even more of a disaster, in a way, this cool seeming upgrade, than the original clunky materialism. Because now nonhumans aren't just lumps, they are blank screens: they have no qualities whatsoever until we've decided what they are. The reductionist upgrade is even more sadistic than the previous version.

Science begins to show us how we contain so much more non-human DNA than human DNA, just to keep us in existence—your bacterial microbiome for instance. We simply can't keep this Severing business up for much longer, can we? But still it marches on, a zombie meme that was untrue at the beginning and is untrue now. Many humanist scholars, hamstrung by the reductionist upgrade I was just describing, still don't want to dirty their hands with such knowledge. It's a disaster for lifeforms—one of whom is ourselves. Retreating to some fictional command module in our thinking heads, cutting the ties to nonhumans in social space, overusing antibacterial soap—it's World War One, and we are both the generals overseeing the battle from afar, and the foot soldiers being mown down in the ploughed up mud.

Maybe one thing that will happen as we admit that nonhumans see us is that we soften those very conceptual categories such as *act* and *behave* or *look* and *see*. Soften them into one another a little bit. Because the categories themselves are based on The Severing. This won't mean that we realize we are all just machines, but that we are haunted by specters or spirits. We don't totally own ourselves, nothing does. I don't know what the new words will be but I think I can see the airport where we're going to land this disastrous plane.

One of the wonderful things about Ed Panar's project is its light touch, its humor. We live in an age in which we deliver ecological information to ourselves with all the subtlety of a Puritan hellfire and brimstone sermon wrapped around a stone and lobbed carelessly through our windows. Enough of this mode already. The mode itself is a PTSD symptom, a symptom of what we have been calling The Severing. Nonhumans seeing me is funny after millennia of telling ourselves that they are unthinking unfeeling machines who couldn't possibly see in the *Avatar* sense. That would imply understanding, we tell ourselves, convinced that thought is what drives perception ("I see," we say, meaning "I understand"), and that thought is the top access mode, the best way, perhaps the only way, of getting at reality.

It's funny—we start to smile. Which is how we begin to cry, for real.

It is a delight to revisit Ed Panar's work, a few years after he kindly introduced it to me. His photographs seem more poignant than ever, now that more of us (the humans) know that we have created an age of mass extinction, only the sixth one on this planet in its four-and-a-half billion year history.

RICE UNIVERSITY, JUNE 2016

Dedicated to Mo

ANIMALS THAT SAW ME: Volume Two

All photographs made by Ed Panar from 1994 to 2016 in
Arizona, Bloomfield Hills, Johnstown, Pittsburgh, Greenpoint,
Round Valley, Garfield, Laurel Highlands, Detroit, and Iceland.

Coordination: Tricia Gabriel, Mike Slack, Jacques Marlow

Distributed in North America by D.A.P. / www.artbook.com

ISBN 978-0-98978597-6
Printed in China

THE ICE PLANT
www.theiceplant.cc